ALL QUIET ON THE ORIENT EXPRESS
'Brilliant, hilariously surreal. Like the Coen
Brothers directing an Alan Bennett play ... fantastic'
Daily Mirror

THE SCHEME FOR FULL EMPLOYMENT
'Imagine *The Office* crossed with
Brave New World ... hilarious'
Daily Express

THE MAINTENANCE OF HEADWAY
'Anyone who has wondered why buses arrive
either in gangs or not at all should find the answer
in Mills' delightful satire about the least reliable
form of public transport' *Daily Mail*

A Cruel Bird Came to
the Nest and Looked In

A Cruel Bird Came to the Nest and Looked In

MAGNUS MILLS

BLOOMSBURY

LONDON · BERLIN · NEW YORK · SYDNEY

First published in Great Britain 2011

Copyright © 2011 by Magnus Mills

The moral right of the author has been asserted

Bloomsbury Publishing Plc
49-51 Bedford Square
London W1CB 3DP

www.bloomsbury.com

Bloomsbury Publishing, London, Berlin, New York and Sydney
A CIP catalogue record for this book is available from the British Library

ISBN 978 1 4088 2120 6 (hardback edition)
ISBN 978 1 4088 2421 4 (trade paperback edition)

10 9 8 7 6 5 4 3 2 1

Typeset by Hewer Text UK Ltd, Edinburgh
Printed in Great Britain by Clays Ltd, St Ives plc

for Sue

1

As the clock struck ten, Smew opened the register.

'Let us begin,' he said. 'Chancellor of the Exchequer?'

'Present,' said Brambling.

'Postmaster General?'

'Present,' said Garganey.

'Astronomer Royal?'

'Here,' said Whimbrel.

'Present,' said Smew.

'Present,' said Whimbrel.

'Comptroller for the Admiralty?'

'Present,' said Sanderling.

'Surveyor of the Imperial Works?'

'Present,' said Dotterel.

'Pellitory-of-the-Wall?'

'Present,' said Wryneck.

'Principal Composer to the Imperial Court?'

'Present,' I said.

'His Exalted Highness, the Majestic Emperor of the

Realms, Dominions, Colonies and Commonwealth of Greater Fallowfields?'

Smew waited but there was no response. We were seated at a round table, with nine chairs spaced evenly apart. One of the chairs was larger and better-upholstered than the others. It was empty. Smew peered at the unoccupied place for a few moments. 'Absent,' he said, putting a cross in the register.

From my position opposite Smew I could see the register upside down. I noticed that this cross was the latest in a long succession of crosses; the rest of us had all received ticks.

There was one further entry to make.

'Librarian-in-Chief?' said Smew.

He inclined his head slightly to acknowledge his own presence, before adding a final tick. Closing the register, he glanced over at the clock.

'We'll wait for a quarter of an hour,' he announced.

So we remained there in silence as fifteen minutes marched slowly by. On my left sat Whimbrel; then came Sanderling, Garganey, the empty chair, Wryneck, Smew, Dotterel and Brambling. On the walls around us hung portraits of several previous emperors; but none, yet, of the new incumbent. The clock stood in the corner of the room. A tasselled cord dangled from the ceiling. Lying on the table were our blank notepads and our pencils. There was nothing else.

After a while Whimbrel began passing the time by drawing circles on his pad, but he ceased when Smew gave him a stern look. Respite came only when the clock chimed the quarter hour. At once the mood lightened considerably.

'Well, now,' said Smew. 'May I suggest we adjourn the meeting? After all, in the absence of His Highness there is very little for us to discuss.'

'Can we assume that this absence is merely temporary?' enquired Wryneck.

'Without doubt,' replied Smew. 'A brief hiatus in the affairs of state; nothing more.'

'Seconded then,' said Wryneck.

'Carried,' said Smew.

The two of them conferred for a short while, then Smew looked across at me and asked, 'Do you know where the cake is?'

'Yes,' I said. 'I took a walk in that direction yesterday afternoon, and again during the evening.'

'Met your troops yet?'

'No. Not yet.'

'In due course, then?'

'Yes.'

'Good.'

Over to my left I thought I sensed Garganey stirring slightly, but he made no comment.

'All done?' said Wryneck, gathering up his notepad and pencil.

This was taken as a signal that the meeting was over. Soon we were all rising to our feet.

'Cabinet resumes next Monday at ten o'clock,' Smew informed us as we dispersed.

I headed out through the door and down the steps, thankful that a conclusion had been reached so quickly. I hadn't got very far, though, when Garganey caught up with me. 'Can I have a word?' he said.

'Certainly.'

'I was just wondering if you kept your card?'

'Yes,' I said. 'As a matter of fact, I'm carrying it with me.'

From my inside pocket I produced a large envelope bearing the words: ON HIS MAJESTY'S IMPERIAL SERVICE.

I handed it to Garganey.

'Thanks,' he said. 'What I'm actually interested in is the postmark. I've only recently taken over as Postmaster General and I've begun studying the workings of the penny post.'

'I didn't know you were new,' I said.

'Oh, yes,' said Garganey. 'I've been in office a comparatively short time.' He examined the postmark closely. 'Ah, thought so.'

'What?'

'Can you remember when this arrived?'

'The day before yesterday,' I said. 'I came straight to court.'

'Well, it was posted more than three weeks ago.'

'Really?'

'See for yourself.'

Garganey handed back the envelope and I looked at the postmark. Sure enough, it was dated almost a month previously.

'Sorry,' I said. 'I never noticed.'

'It's not your fault,' he said. 'Obviously the postmen have been shirking some of their obligations.'

'So it appears.'

'I'll have to see what can be done.'

4

I returned the envelope to my pocket.

'Right,' I said, preparing to move on. 'I'll bid you good-day then.'

Garganey stood staring distractedly into the distance. He plainly had something further on his mind.

Then he said, 'Smew's got a bit of a cheek, hasn't he?'

'How do you mean?' I asked.

'Taking over the meeting the way he did.'

'Well,' I said, 'I suppose somebody had to.'

'That's twice in two weeks.'

'Oh, I didn't know that.'

'Then there was all that questioning you about the cake: it's none of his damned business!'

'To tell the truth,' I said, 'I wasn't really bothered.'

'That's not the point,' said Garganey. 'Smew is Librarian-in-Chief: he holds no other title. Simply because he's been here the longest doesn't authorise him to lord it over the rest of us. We're all officers of the empire and we're all equal in the hierarchy. It's not up to him to conduct cabinet meetings.'

'Well, hopefully His Majesty will be back next week,' I ventured. 'By the way, do we know where he is, exactly?'

'No,' said Garganey. 'The formal explanation is "temporarily absent", which could of course mean anything.'

While we were talking I spotted Whimbrel go wandering towards the observatory. He'd asked me earlier if I'd like to go up and have a look around the place, so after making my excuses to Garganey I set off in pursuit.

The observatory stood in some parkland at the top of a grassy hill, slightly isolated from the rest of the royal court. The approach was via a long, curving path followed by a steep flight of steps. When I arrived at the door I found Whimbrel fumbling with his keys.

'Oh, hello,' he said, as I joined him. 'Glad you could come. I saw you talking to Garganey but I didn't want to interrupt.'

'Did you know he was a recent arrival as well?' I enquired.

'No, I didn't,' answered Whimbrel. 'That makes three of us then.'

He found the correct key and unlocked the door. Once inside, we climbed an iron staircase until we came at last to a large octagonal room with tall, narrow windows.

'Here we are,' he said. 'Welcome to my domain.'

On a table were some huge charts, all lying on top of one another in complete disarray. Closer inspection revealed that they were maps of the stars.

'These should be useful,' I remarked.

'Indeed,' said Whimbrel. 'Frankly, I've no idea how I'd manage without them. All the stars look identical to me.'

'I'm sure you'll learn them after a while,' I said. 'Fortunately, they're all fixed in their constellations, so once you know them you probably won't forget.'

I went to a window and gazed out.

'They're all fixed, are they?' said Whimbrel. 'Well, that's definitely a fact worth knowing. Thank you.'

'My pleasure,' I replied. 'Tell you what, why don't I come back this evening and we can have a proper look?'

'If you really don't mind.'

'Of course not.'

'That would be most helpful.'

'Mind you,' I said, 'I'm surprised you haven't got a telescope.'

'Oh, there is a telescope,' said Whimbrel. 'It's up on the roof.'

'Ah.'

'Doesn't work though.'

'It must do,' I said. 'You're the Astronomer Royal.'

'I assure you it doesn't.'

'Show me.'

'Very well,' said Whimbrel, 'if you insist.'

At the top of the staircase was a ladder that went up through an aperture in the ceiling. Whimbrel led the way and a minute later we opened a tiny door to emerge on to the flat roof of the building. There, perched on a stone pillar, was a telescope. It appeared to be a substantial piece of equipment, housed in a thick metal casing and painted bright blue. When I looked into the eyepiece, however, I could see nothing; nor would the telescope move when I tried to alter its angle. Instead, it remained locked in the same position, aimed at a point somewhere below the horizon. As such, it was entirely unsuitable for the purposes of astronomy.

'See what I mean?' said Whimbrel.

'Yes,' I said. 'Can't you get anything done about it?'

'I don't really know who to ask.'

'Why don't you try Dotterel? He's in charge of all the artisans: he told me that himself. Surely he'll know what to do.'

'Good idea. Yes, I'll have to ask him next time I see him.'

I laid my hand flat on the telescope.

'This must have had at least ten coats of paint,' I said.

'Not recently,' said Whimbrel.

'No,' I agreed. 'Not recently.'

'It must be to protect it from the weather.'

We both looked up at the sky, which was pale and colourless. Autumn was clearly drawing near.

'I wonder what I'm supposed to do on cloudy evenings,' said Whimbrel. 'I won't be able to perform my duties properly if I can't see anything.'

'What are your duties,' I enquired, 'in a nutshell?'

'Not sure really,' he answered. 'As far as I know there aren't any definitive rules.'

'Maybe you're expected simply to contemplate the firmament,' I suggested. 'A sort of celestial night watchman.'

'You make it sound like a holiday job,' said Whimbrel.

'No, no,' I said, 'I'm fully aware that we all enjoy highly exalted posts. Some might even call us privileged to be as close as we are to the emperor. All the same I can't help speculating whether our roles aren't merely ceremonial. I mean to say, exactly how seriously are we meant to take them?'

'I'm not sure,' he said. 'I've received no guidance on the matter.'

'Nor me.'

'I understand it's customary in the empire to grant positions of high office to people who know little about their subject; in my case the custom is being maintained to the letter.'

'Same here,' I said. 'I've just been appointed Principal Composer to the Imperial Court, yet all I know about music theory is what I've taught myself from books.'

'That's better than nothing,' said Whimbrel.

'Only marginally,' I replied.

He dwelt on this for a while, and then asked, 'What do you make of the others?'

'In the cabinet?'

'Yes.'

'They're certainly a mixed bunch,' I said. 'The only one I've spoken to at any length so far is Garganey, and he seems to be very fastidious about his work. He's already begun an investigation into the penny post to see if he can get it operating more efficiently.'

'He'll be lucky,' said Whimbrel. 'An inefficient postal system is another of those unwavering imperial customs. What always confounds me is how items of mail come to be lost in the post.'

'Don't ask me.'

'How can a physical entity disappear inside an abstract entity?'

'That remains one of the great imponderable questions.'

'Precisely.'

'To be fair, though, most lost items do turn up after a while.

Oh, by the way, talking about items of mail, did you keep your card?'

'Indeed I did!' exclaimed Whimbrel. 'In fact I must show you. Come on! Follow me!'

We abandoned the telescope and went back down into the observatory. He indicated a picture frame on the wall. Displayed inside was a card similar to the one I'd received two days ago. The wording was slightly different to mine. It read:

BY COMMAND OF

HIS EXALTED HIGHNESS

THE MAJESTIC EMPEROR OF THE REALMS, DOMINIONS,

COLONIES AND COMMONWEALTH

OF

GREATER FALLOWFIELDS

YOU ARE SUMMONED FORTHWITH

TO THE

IMPERIAL COURT

WHERE YOU WILL ASSUME THE OFFICE OF

ASTRONOMER ROYAL.

The picture frame had been finished in gold, which perfectly matched the ornate lettering on the card.

'Very smart,' I said. 'Maybe I should get mine framed as well.'

'It makes you realise the responsibility bestowed on us,' said Whimbrel. 'We're part of an elite cohort.'

'Quite.'

'A motley one, nevertheless,' he continued. 'Whoever would have guessed that the imperial cabinet included an astronomer? Or even a composer?'

'Actually, I think it's all rather neatly balanced,' I said. 'Not too much emphasis on any particular aspect of life.'

'Good point.'

'Furthermore, you'll notice that there's absolutely no kind of spiritual, theological or pastoral representative.'

'Thank God,' remarked Whimbrel.

2

What I really wanted was to have the cake to myself. When I approached, however, I could hear music playing. This told me I would not be alone. I stopped and listened. They were rehearsing the imperial anthem again, just as they had been on the previous day. Casually, I wondered whether this was the only tune they knew; then I told myself not to be so churlish. Such an attitude would hardly help matters, especially at this early stage. Despite being their superior, I had to remember that I was utterly dependent on them, at least for the time being. Therefore, like any good commander, I should start by trying to learn from my subordinates. With these thoughts in mind I advanced once more towards my destination.

The cake was probably the most famous landmark in all of Fallowfields. People were known to journey from the provinces simply to gaze upon its exquisite proportions. What a sight it was! Situated amongst the trees at the edge of the royal park, it looked almost good enough to eat. The cake was a perfectly round building with smooth yellow walls rising to a creamy-white domed roof. A veritable essay in the imperial style, it was apparently at its most splendid when bathed in sunshine during long, languid, summer afternoons. Indeed, the walls were of such a rich hue that the more rustic visitors firmly believed they were made from marzipan.

The truth was hardly less exotic. Constructed in the days when the empire was at its zenith, the cake was built from a very rare kind of stone, quarried to specification in a faraway land and ferried home in ships. It took twenty-three years to carry out the work, from design to completion.

I paused at the door and listened. The music I could hear was even louder than before. The imperial anthem, having galloped at full pelt to the end of its glorious refrain, now returned again to the beginning of the verse. And so it went on: verse and refrain, verse and refrain, seemingly for ever and ever.

The door was massive, and made from oak. Above it was a cast-iron fanlight. I turned the handle and pushed the door open. The music ceased. I pulled the door to and the music resumed, a little raggedly at first, but quickly regaining its former unison, taking up the anthem at the point where it had broken off.

I repeated the exercise, pushing the door open and causing the music to stop, then closing it once more. As the music started yet again I sensed I could not keep on interrupting them like this. On the other hand, I had no intention of waiting meekly outside. Accordingly, I took a deep breath, swung the door open and marched in.

'Carry on!' I ordered, in a breezy manner.

The imperial anthem had already begun grinding to a halt for a third time, but my confident instruction was enough to set it going again. I saw that I had entered a large auditorium. Down below me sat an orchestra about ninety strong, arrayed in a half-circle before an empty podium.

'Good!' I called out encouragingly, although I doubted if they could hear me any longer. The music proceeded unabated, and was now terrifically loud. I strode quickly down the centre aisle, then passed amongst the musicians and mounted three steps on to the podium. I turned to face them just as the refrain came to a close and the main theme was due to start all over again. When this moment actually arrived I felt my hair stand on end. We were off once more at full tilt, but this time I was in command! I looked about me. To my left sat row upon row of violins, violas and oboes; in front of me were bassoons and yet more woodwind; and to my right were trombones, trumpets, horns and tubas, as well as all the lower strings. Beyond these were ranged kettledrums, snares, a bass drum, a great gong, some bells and many other kinds of percussion. There was also a harp.

The orchestra played on. I soon discovered that all I had to do was wave my hands vaguely in time to the music, and they in turn would keep time with me. It all seemed very easy. After a while, however, I noticed that the musicians were not actually following my lead. Without exception their eyes were focused on a violinist who sat at the end of the front row immediately to my left. His chair was positioned slightly forward and turned at an angle to the others, and this allowed the entire orchestra to see him. Carefully, I observed his actions. I soon saw that he was hardly bothering to play his violin: instead, he concentrated all his efforts on keeping time with his right hand (in which he also held his bow). I continued watching in fascination as we charged again through the tireless anthem. At one point this violinist caught my gaze. I gave him a nod of acknowledgement and he returned the gesture deferentially. He appeared to have the orchestra under his total control.

Nonetheless I was their supreme leader by appointment, so I went on 'conducting' in my own style for several more rounds of music. At the same time I took the opportunity to appraise my new charges, if only broadly. They were all dressed in the imperial livery: frock coats of black velvet with scarlet frogging, and black breeches. These outfits, I noted, were spotlessly clean but rather threadbare. Their boots were black with brass buckles. The violinist on my left was attired no differently from his colleagues. They were all playing without scores on their music stands, presumably because the anthem was quite familiar to each of them. A painstaking count told me that there were ninety-eight musicians altogether. Standing nearby, unused, was a piano.

At last I decided it was time for a break. Only then did it occur to me that I had no idea how to stop them. I ceased waving my hands but nothing happened; likewise when I clapped them together. The orchestra just kept on going, such was their level of absorption. Fortunately, the 'lead' violinist seemed to understand my dilemma because suddenly, at a signal from him, the music came to an abrupt halt. Then, to my surprise, they all rose to their feet and bowed to me.

An awkward silence followed as they stood holding their various instruments.

'All right,' I said. 'Thank you.'

There was no response.

'You can sit down,' I said. 'Have a rest.'

Quietly, they all sat down, but still the silence prevailed. Perhaps, I thought, they felt intimidated by my presence on the podium, towering above them as it were. For this reason I stepped down and strolled over to the violinist in the front row. Instantly, he stood up and bowed again.

'Your name is?' I asked.

'Greylag, sir.'

'And how long have you been with the orchestra?'

My question, intended merely to establish a less formal tone, appeared instead to baffle Greylag completely. He was clearly lost for words. It then dawned on me that such an enquiry would be meaningless to him and his companions. The imperial orchestra of Fallowfields was comprised wholly of serfs, and hence they knew of no existence other than their service to the court. To ask Greylag how long he'd been with the orchestra was as futile as asking him about his expectations for the future. My mistake, of course, had been to forget the lowliness of his situation. True enough, serfdom was a rare circumstance nowadays in Greater Fallowfields, persisting mostly in the farthest-flung corners of the colonies. Here at the very heart of the empire, by contrast, the tradition remained fully intact. These particular serfs had the distinction of being the personal property of the emperor himself. My question, therefore, verged on foolishness.

Even so, it was too late now. As Greylag stood mute before me I realised that there was still much for me to learn.

'Sorry, sir,' he murmured at length. 'I don't know the answer.'

'That's all right, Greylag,' I said. 'Maybe we should have some more music.'

'Yes, sir. Thank you, sir,' he said.

'Oh, by the way,' I added, 'is there anything else, apart from the imperial anthem?'

'Well, we do have some variations on the theme, sir, if you're interested.'

I wasn't sure what he meant exactly, but the suggestion sounded fairly reasonable so I gave my immediate consent. I was then treated to a performance of the same tune played in countless different ways. Again, I 'conducted' from the podium while Greylag took care of the actual details. I was now beginning to recognise the full potential of this arrangement. Indeed, my first day in charge of the orchestra had turned out to be most satisfactory.

Eventually, when afternoon drifted into evening, I left them to their own devices and headed for the door. As I walked across the park I could still hear the music ringing in my ears, and I reflected on how extraordinary it was that a single theme could be subject to so many modifications and still be recognisable. At one point even the melody itself seemed to have been altered, yet the music retained the unmistakable stamp of the imperial anthem. I looked forward with eager anticipation to yet further variations. Moreover, it was plain that I had the finest orchestral resources at my disposal. All I had to do now was work out precisely what I was going to do with them.

It was a chilly evening and the stars were out. I peered up and verified the positions of one or two constellations that I knew; then I strolled on towards the observatory which, I noticed, was in complete darkness. For a moment I assumed that Whimbrel had wandered off somewhere, but when I arrived at the door I found it was unlocked. I went inside and ascended the iron spiral, my boots clanging noisily on the stairway. Then I heard Whimbrel's voice from above.

'Come up!' he called. 'Sorry, it's so gloomy!'

I found him standing near a window, struggling to read one of his charts by starlight. He turned it this way and that, but appeared to be having no success.

'This is impossible,' he said. 'To observe the stars properly it needs to be dark; but when it's dark, of course, I can't tell what it says on the chart.'

'Why don't you go up on the roof?' I suggested.

'I've tried that,' replied Whimbrel. 'It's hardly any better up there.'

'Well, I know a couple of constellations to start you off,' I said. 'How about if I point them out and then you can check them against the chart tomorrow in daylight?'

Whimbrel agreed to my proposal and we went up the ladder to the roof. When we emerged through the tiny door we were confronted once again by the defunct telescope.

'Incidentally,' said Whimbrel, 'I had a word with Dotterel this afternoon.'

'Oh, yes?'

'He said he couldn't help.'

'Why not?' I demanded. 'He's supposed to be in charge of all the artisans: he told me that himself.'

'Yes, he told me that as well,' said Whimbrel. 'Nevertheless, he said he had nobody on his books who knew about telescopes.'

'I see.'

'There's more,' confided Whimbrel, speaking more quietly now. 'According to Dotterel, all offices of state are separate bodies and should have no involvement with one another.'

'Really?'

'He was quite insistent on the matter. As far as Dotterel is concerned his only obligation is to the emperor himself.'

'Well, that's fair enough,' I said. 'Clearly, his loyalties lie in the right direction.'

'Of course,' said Whimbrel. 'Service to the empire is paramount. Even so, it seems a great shame that he's apparently ruled out any form of co-operation between departments.'

Privately, I concurred with Whimbrel. I could see little to be gained, however, from openly taking sides against Dotterel. Admittedly, I had found his boasts about being in charge of all the artisans irritating to say the least. It struck me that such claims required further testing; hence, for the time being I would continue to give Dotterel the benefit of the doubt. Hopefully, Whimbrel could be persuaded to forget the entire episode.

'Right then,' I said, glancing up at the sky. 'I think it's probably best to begin with the Plough.'

The seven stars in question were easily recognisable. They appeared to have been placed there for the very purpose of tutoring Whimbrel in the basics of astronomy. Dutifully he wrote the word 'plough' on his notepad; then he stood gazing at the formation as if trying to fix it in his memory. Whimbrel's disclosure that he knew little about his subject was obviously an understatement. Idly, I pondered what might happen if I told him that the sky was an immense heavenly vault which lay resting on the earth's rim? He'd most likely believe me and copy my description on to his notepad. The outcome of such a jape, I quickly realised, could be disastrous, especially if the assertion went on to win imperial approval. After all, Whimbrel was the Astronomer Royal. It was not a role to be toyed with, and consequently I decided only to relate a few, indisputable facts. The rest he would have to learn on his own.

Once he'd mastered the Plough I was able to show him how to identify the Pole Star.

'Then you'll know where north is,' I explained.

'Why do I need to know that?' Whimbrel enquired.

'Believe me, it's important,' I said. 'Besides, someone might ask you.'

'Who?'

'Someone who wants to go there.'

'You mean by ship?'

'Yes, possibly, or even overland.'

'Who, though?'

Whimbrel was evidently unimpressed by the whole notion of 'the north'.

'All right,' I said, changing tack. 'What if the emperor asks you where north is? What will you do then?'

'Oh, yes,' said Whimbrel, 'I never thought of that.'

'He could ask you anything. It's quite possible he might turn up here at the observatory and demand a guided tour. Just because he's missed a few cabinet meetings doesn't necessarily mean he's entirely indisposed.'

'No, I suppose not,' conceded Whimbrel. 'All the same, it's a little odd that nobody's seen him lately.'

'Yes, it is,' I agreed, 'very odd.'

'So you think he's gone off travelling in the north, do you?'

'No, no,' I said. 'That was a hypothetical example. For all we know he could still be here at court.'

'All they're saying is he's "temporarily absent".'

'Who are "they"?' I asked.

'You know,' said Whimbrel. 'Officialdom.'

'But we're officialdom,' I said. 'Me, you and the other six officers-of-state. There's no one else.'

Whimbrel made no further comment, and instead stood in silence as if contemplating for the very first time the full weight of his responsibilities. The evening had passed quickly, and as we watched we began to witness the lamps being turned down in the royal quarter. From here on the observatory roof we could see across the park to the great library, the general post office, the admiralty building, the counting house and the ministry of works. They were mostly in darkness now, with only the occasional glimmer of light remaining here and there. I noticed that the cake, too, was unlit. Presumably, this meant the music had stopped at last.

'I think that's enough for one day,' I said, so we made our way back down the iron ladder.

'Have you heard about these talks that Smew gives once a fortnight?' said Whimbrel.

'No,' I replied. 'What are they about?'

'The history of the empire, apparently. We're supposed to go to the reading room of the great library if we're interested: every other Wednesday afternoon at three o'clock.'

'Oh, well, I might have a look in,' I said. 'They could be quite informative.'

'I don't like history,' said Whimbrel. 'It's boring.'

'It depends how it's presented,' I countered. 'Why don't you come along and give it a try?'

'All right,' he said. 'If you're going, I'll go.'

Before leaving I happened to glance out of the window one last time.

'Now there's a sight to behold,' I said. 'Look at Jupiter.'

Whimbrel joined me at the window and together we admired Jupiter's bright presence high in the southern sky.

'Marvellous,' he said. 'Now I must write that down straight away. Where's my notepad?'

Whimbrel had mislaid it somewhere. He was still conducting a search when I said goodnight and departed. I was coming through the door at the bottom of the stairway when I heard him call down from above.

'Did you say Neptune?'

'No,' I called back. 'Jupiter.'

'Ah yes, Jupiter. Goodnight then.'

'Goodnight.'

It occurred to me that this wasn't actually 'goodnight' for Whimbrel: rather, it was only the beginning of his working day. A long and lonely vigil lay ahead.

For my part, I intended to take advantage of the lateness of the hour and catch up on some much-needed piano practice. This was necessary, I'd concluded, if I was to fulfil my duties correctly. After all, who'd ever heard of a composer who couldn't play anything?

The cake reared out of the gloom. I entered via the main door and wandered down into the orchestra pit, where I was pleased to see a light glowing dimly over the piano. All the other instruments, I noticed, had been tidied away in their cases. I turned the light up slightly, then sat down and played the chord of G major a few times, just to get started. Next I went through a series of major and minor scales, arpeggios and broken chords. These all went fine until I attempted to play some major scales in contrary motion. As usual I got stuck halfway and had to begin again. When I got stuck for a third time I gave up and sat there striking random notes. This reminded me that I ought to find some proper pieces of music to try. Maybe I should consult with Greylag on the matter the next day. I was about to resume the minor scales when I heard a quiet murmur coming from somewhere behind me. I looked around and saw nothing, but when I turned the light up further I realised there were figures lurking at the back of the auditorium.

'Who's there?' I demanded.

'Pardon us, sir,' came the reply. 'We didn't mean to disturb you.'

The voice belonged to Greylag. I walked up and found a large proportion of the orchestra sitting in three rows of hard seats.

'What are you doing here?' I asked.

'Waiting to go to sleep, sir,' said Greylag.

'What do you mean "waiting"?'

'Well, sir,' he said, 'we've only got one bed between us, so we all have to take our turns.'

'Show me,' I ordered.

Greylag led me beyond the orchestra pit to an antechamber. Inside was a broad wooden cot in which a dozen cellos lay side by side, all fast asleep.

'The bassoons have their turn next, sir,' explained Greylag, 'followed by the trumpets and trombones.'

'And meanwhile you all sit waiting in the hard seats?'

'Yes, sir.'

'Then why don't you use the soft seats at the front?' I enquired. 'Surely, they'd be much more comfortable.'

'It's not allowed,' said Greylag.

'Whyever not?'

'I'm not sure, sir.'

'Right!' I snapped. 'Not allowed, eh? Well, we'll soon see about that!'

I marched hurriedly to the main door where a notice-board in an alcove displayed various rules and regulations pertaining to the cake. I read through them and then walked back.

'You're quite correct, Greylag,' I said. 'You're not allowed in the soft seats.'

'No, sir.'

'Unfortunately, you're not allowed in the hard ones either,' I continued. 'They're all reserved for commoners.'

A doleful look crossed Greylag's face, but he said nothing.

'I'm sorry, Greylag,' I said. 'Rules are rules.'

In the subdued hush that followed I went over to the piano. I sat down and began working my way through the minor scales again, one by one, until, predictably, I got stuck.

'May I, sir?'

I glanced to my left and saw Greylag standing nearby. Something in his manner suggested he wanted to help me, so I inclined my head a little and waited.

'If the thumb is allowed to pass underneath the forefinger,' he said, 'then the hand is able to flow more freely along the keyboard.'

He demonstrated by playing a brief chromatic scale; then I tried the same technique. Sure enough, this made it all seem much easier.

'Thank you, Greylag,' I said. 'So you play violin *and* piano, do you?'

'Yes, sir,' he answered.

'Come on then,' I said, rising from the piano stool. 'Let's hear a tune.'

Greylag took my place obediently. For a moment he sat with his hands poised over the keys; then he began to play a gentle, lilting piece of a kind I had never heard before. After a few bars he stopped.

'What sort of music was that?' I asked.

'It was a cradle song, sir,' said Greylag.

'You mean a lullaby?'

'Yes, sir.'

'I see.'

Somewhere in the distance a clock struck midnight. I'd forgotten how late it was. I looked towards the antechamber where the cellos lay sleeping. The other musicians remained huddled at the back of the hall.

'All right, Greylag,' I said, 'I'll come back in the morning.'

Without another word I left the cake and walked back towards the palace gates. All was quiet. Darkness had fallen on the capital, and almost every building I passed was bathed in shadows.

There was one exception, however. Eventually I turned a corner and came upon the Maypole. As always, coloured lights were shining brightly behind the frosted windows. A welcoming lantern swung from the lintel. The door was closed, but beyond it I could hear laughter, snatches of songs, and the tinkling of glasses. Wood smoke was drifting from the chimney, and I imagined there to be a huge log fire blazing in the hearth. For a few minutes I stood listening to the sounds of merrymaking. I thought about going in, but then I decided it could wait until another evening.

3

'Absent,' said Smew.

Once again he had taken it upon himself to mark the register; and once again there was no sign of the emperor. I couldn't see whether Smew had inserted a cross or a tick, because today he was holding the register tilted slightly towards him. Only Wryneck, who sat immediately to his right, had an unobstructed view.

'We'll wait for a quarter of an hour,' Smew announced.

So again we sat around the table in silence as fifteen minutes went by. As usual, we all had our notepads in front of us. There was also a small stack of textbooks positioned between Wryneck and Smew. They all looked identical, but from where I was sitting I was unable to see the title. Eventually, the clock chimed the quarter hour.

'Well, now,' said Smew, finally closing the register. 'Is there any other business?'

Nobody spoke.

'I'm surprised,' Smew remarked. 'Doesn't the Postmaster General have anything to report, for example?'

'Actually, I do have some findings to relate,' said Garganey, 'but I can hardly proceed without the emperor's consent.'

'His Majesty's absence is merely temporary,' said Wryneck. 'Besides which, you could always present a provisional report to cabinet.'

'Seconded,' said Smew.

'Carried,' said Wryneck.

The clock ticked. Garganey stared frostily across the table at Wryneck. To my left, Whimbrel shuffled his feet uneasily.

'All right,' said Garganey at length. 'I can't see any harm in a "provisional report" as you so neatly put it.'

'Thank you,' said Smew. 'I'm sure it will be appreciated by all of us.'

A murmur of agreement went around the table. Garganey glanced briefly at his notes. Then he began.

'Now, as you know, we have for many years been suffering delays in the postal service. Letters posted just around the corner can take three or four days to arrive, whilst those sent to the provinces tend to turn up several weeks later, even when they bear the imperial seal. Hitherto, such delays have been viewed as intrinsic to the postal system, the general assumption being that they are largely unavoidable.' Garganey paused momentarily before continuing. 'My recent studies, however, have shown that this is not quite the case. There is, in fact, a simple explanation: namely, the postmen's custom of stopping halfway through the morning and coming back for breakfast.'

Smew sat bolt upright in his chair. 'Is this true?' he demanded.

'I'm afraid so,' said Garganey. 'Breakfast is regarded as sacrosanct amongst the postmen. Even if they're miles away, they always come back.'

'What do they do after breakfast?' asked Brambling.

'They resume their deliveries,' replied Garganey. 'Oh, there's no doubt they pursue the task earnestly. They set off with fully laden sacks and a cheery greeting for everyone they meet. The trouble is they only work until noon, which means that some of the mail doesn't reach its destination.'

'What happens to it?'

'Any remaining letters go back in the pillar boxes to be collected the following day.'

'In other words the post is delayed,' said Smew.

'Precisely,' said Garganey, folding away his notes and looking around the table. 'The solution, gentlemen, is obvious.'

'Well, you can't stop them having breakfast,' said Brambling. 'It's the most important meal of the day.'

'Of course not,' conceded Garganey. 'I wouldn't dream of it. Furthermore, important changes cannot be enacted without the express approval of His Majesty. In his temporary absence, therefore, I would like to suggest a trial period during which the postmen have their breakfast before they leave in the morning.'

'What time would that be?' enquired Brambling. 'Roughly.'

'About five o'clock,' said Garganey.

'Is that seven days a week?'

'Six.'

As the discussion continued, I quietly wondered whether Garganey would be able to face a hearty breakfast at that time in the morning. Surely, the whole point of the postmen going out early was so that they could get some work behind them while building up a decent appetite. It struck me that Garganey's proposition was bound to cause more problems than it solved. As far as I was concerned, interfering with a man's breakfast went beyond the pale. I didn't say anything, however. Garganey would have to find out for himself.

A trial period of three months was generally agreed, and I then expected deliberations to be swiftly concluded. Smew, though, had one more item for us to consider.

'Now then,' he said, 'I know that it's only the beginning of autumn and the twelve-day feast still seems a long way away. All the same, this is the time of year when we need to start thinking about some kind of courtly entertainment for the occasion. Sooner or later His Majesty is bound to send us an official reminder, but meanwhile it would be a great help if we could all at least mull over a few ideas.'

'What about some dancing girls?' suggested Sanderling.

Smew peered across the table at Sanderling as if he'd never noticed him before.

'You were very quick off the mark,' he said. 'Dancing girls, eh? Well, that certainly rings a bell.'

From the ceiling there dangled a tasselled cord. Smew pulled it and an instant later a liveried attendant came into the room.

'Yes, sir?'

'Ah, Shrike,' said Smew. 'Whatever happened to those dancing girls we used to have?'

'They went away, sir.'

'Why was that?'

'They became great with child, sir.'

'All of them?'

'I'm afraid so, sir.'

'Do we know . . .?'

'No, sir.'

'I see.' Smew furrowed his brow. 'All right, Shrike. That will be all for now.'

The attendant nodded and left the room, closing the door behind him. The rest of us sat in silence for several seconds, until eventually Garganey spoke. 'Since when have we had liveried attendants at our beck and call?'

'Actually, there's only one of them,' Smew replied. 'Shrike has been helping me out as Assistant Librarian.'

'Really?' said Garganey. He appeared unimpressed.

'It looks as though there won't be any dancing girls,' remarked Wryneck.

'Indeed not,' said Smew, 'and to be honest they probably wouldn't have been entirely suitable for a courtly entertainment. What I had in mind was some sort of performance in which we ourselves could participate.'

'You mean a play, for instance?' said Wryneck.

'Correct,' said Smew. 'Obviously it would need to be one that accommodated all eight of us more or less equally. I've taken the liberty of bringing along an example that just might fit the bill.' He reached for the textbooks which were stacked beside him and began handing them around. 'Unfortunately there are only six copies available, so some of you will have to share.'

Whimbrel took one of the books and placed it between himself and me.

'Ah, yes, I've heard of this,' he said, examining the title page. 'They all get killed at the end, don't they?'

'A few of them, not all,' said Smew. 'However, there is no need to concern ourselves with the details of the plot at this juncture. Instead, I thought perhaps we could simply read through one of the scenes in order to get a feel of the play. Also, we might get some idea as to who will be suited to what parts.'

'It doesn't look to be a very long play,' observed Brambling.

'That's a point in its favour,' said Smew. 'The entire five acts only take about an hour and a half all told, which is quite a lot less than the average cabinet meeting. In fact, we could rehearse the play while we're waiting for His Majesty to reappear.'

Dotterel had already begun flicking through his copy of the book. 'Who's going to play the king then?' he enquired.

'I was coming to that,' Smew replied. 'There's a famous scene in the play involving a banquet, so I suggest that since we're all sitting around this table we should give it a try, each of us taking turns to be different characters.'

During the ongoing discussions I'd been expecting an outburst from Garganey at any moment. After all, Smew had seized the helm again, just like on the previous Monday. I could tell from Garganey's face that he had little enthusiasm for joining in with Smew's project, but to my surprise he didn't offer a word of objection. He merely sat at the table studying his copy of the book.

'The scene in question is on page forty-three,' said Smew. 'Now all you need to know for the time being is that the king is the only person at the banquet who cannot see the ghost. Perhaps we could start by reading it silently to ourselves.'

We all obeyed.

Whimbrel, I soon discovered, had the habit of running his index finger along each line of print, word by word, as he read. Presumably he thought that I would read at precisely the same pace as him while we were sharing, whereas in truth I went fairly quickly and had to keep waiting until he moved his finger out of the way. Still, we managed somehow, reaching the end of the scene after only a few minutes. The first to finish, though, was Dotterel.

'This ghost,' he said. 'Who is he, exactly?'

'He's a former friend of the king,' answered Smew.

'But he can't see him?'

'No.'

'Right.' Dotterel turned back to page forty-three and commenced reading the scene again.

In the meantime, Smew addressed the rest of us. 'You'll notice that one of the characters is a lady,' he said. 'To save unnecessary embarrassment I'll take her part for now. Unless someone else wishes to volunteer, of course?'

Nobody did.

'I'll be the ghost,' said Whimbrel.

'I'll be the king,' said Garganey, 'if nobody minds.'

'And I'll be the murderer,' said Sanderling.

'All right,' said Smew. 'Everyone else will be the noble guests. Now to begin with the king has to "mingle with society and play the humble host", which means basically that he has to walk around the table greeting everybody. So, when you're ready, Garganey.'

'Just a second,' Dotterel interjected. 'Shouldn't we move the emperor's chair out of the way?'

'Why's that?' asked Smew.

'Well, the king says "the table's full".'

'So?'

'It can't really be full when there's an empty chair, can it?'

'It won't be empty for very long,' said Smew, 'because the ghost comes and sits in it.'

'But you just said the king couldn't see the ghost.'

'Correct.'

'So it'll still look empty to the king.'

'And whilst I'm walking around the table,' added Garganey, 'my chair's going to be empty too.'

'That's two empty chairs,' said Whimbrel.

'All right!' snapped Smew, closing his book and laying it on the table. 'You've all made it quite clear you're not interested in doing this play, so we won't bother!'

'On the contrary,' said Dotterel. 'I think it seems very profound on first reading. I'm definitely for carrying on.'

35

'Same here,' said Brambling.

'Why don't we simply pretend that the emperor's chair isn't there?' I suggested. 'After all, we're hardly entitled to move it out of the way.'

One or two people murmured their assent.

'Sounds like a reasonable compromise,' said Smew. 'Everyone agreed?'

'Agreed,' said Wryneck.

The clock struck eleven.

'Is that the time already?' said Sanderling.

No one answered.

'Maybe we should leave it until another day,' I said. 'Then we can all read the play at our leisure and come back next week fully prepared.'

'Good idea,' said Brambling.

'Well, I suppose there's no particular hurry,' observed Smew, 'just so long as everybody does their homework properly.'

'We'll do our best,' said Garganey. 'I presume I'll be king again next time?'

'If you like,' said Smew.

For an instant I thought I saw the pair of them glance warily at one another across the table; but then I decided it was probably only my imagination. Nonetheless an awkward silence ensued, during which the rest of us began rising to our feet. Sanderling went over to the clock and stood gazing through the glass at its inner workings. He seemed slightly startled when all of a sudden the minute hand ticked forward by one degree.

'Can we take these books with us?' asked Whimbrel.

'I'm afraid not,' said Smew. 'You'll have to come to the great library and read them there.'

'But I thought libraries were for borrowing books.'

'It's not a public lending library,' Smew replied. 'It's the imperial library of the court of Greater Fallowfields. There's an important difference.'

'Sorry,' said Whimbrel. 'I'll try to bear it in mind.'

Wryneck gathered together the books and handed them to Smew. Meanwhile, I headed out through the door and down the steps, thankful that the meeting was over for another week. I hadn't got very far, however, when Brambling caught up with me.

'Can I have a word?' he said.

4

The counting house was tall and narrow and built from red brick. Brambling unlocked the front door and led me inside.

'Here we are,' he said. 'Welcome to my domain.'

We were in a plainly decorated room with small windows and sparse furnishings. There was a marble floor, a desk and two chairs. In the corner stood an iron-bound treasure chest. A huge ledger lay on top of the desk. On the walls hung portraits of several previous emperors; but none, yet, of the latest incumbent.

'Three words actually,' said Brambling. 'Fees, rents and disbursements.'

'Do I owe some rent then?' I enquired.

'Oh no,' he said. 'Officers-of-state reside at the emperor's expense.'

'That's what I thought.'

'The reason I've invited you here is to discuss your stipend.'

'Ah.'

'I expect you're curious to learn what it is, aren't you?'

'To tell you the truth I hadn't really considered it.'

'I'm surprised,' remarked Brambling. 'All the others have been here to claim theirs already.'

'Even Whimbrel?'

'Yes.'

'Well, he never said anything to me about it.'

'There's no reason why he should, is there?'

'No,' I said, 'I suppose not.'

'Anyway, please take a seat and we'll look it up.'

We sat down opposite one another at the desk and Brambling opened the ledger. It was evidently a weighty tome because at his first attempt to turn its pages it slammed shut again noisily. The sound reverberated all around the counting house. Only when I reached over and helped from my side of the desk was Brambling able to open the ledger properly and find the place he required. I could see a series of printed columns with handwritten entries beside them.

'Now then,' said Brambling, running his finger down the page. 'Principal Composer to the Imperial Court. According to my records the office pays a stipend of sixpence.'

'Very generous,' I said.

From where I sat I could clearly see the entries for all the other officers-of-state, including Brambling himself. Each was to receive a stipend of sixpence, just the same as me. Brambling must have known this beforehand and hence there had been no real need for him to 'look it up'. I didn't mention this, though, as I had no wish to quash Brambling's pretensions. In his role as Chancellor of the Exchequer he dealt with all fees, rents and disbursements, and it was his privilege to conduct matters in the way he thought appropriate.

Carefully, he closed the ledger. Next he opened a drawer on his side of the desk and from it produced a tin money box. This, apparently, was locked. Brambling then proceeded to fumble in his pockets until eventually he found the key. Lastly he opened the lid and took out a sixpence, which he placed on the desk before me.

'Thanks,' I said. 'Do I need to sign for this?'

'Of course not,' replied Brambling. 'Your office is one of trust.'

I took the sixpence and examined it casually.

'Just one more question,' I continued. 'Is it sixpence a day or sixpence a week?'

At these words Brambling looked at me with complete astonishment. It was as if I had just queried a central tenet of his existence; or challenged the integrity of the chancellery; or maybe suggested that the counting house was built on shifting sands. For several long moments he stared at me silently across his desk. Then he stood up and walked around the room, glancing from time to time in my direction. Finally, he opened the door, went outside and peered in at me through the window.

After a while he came back.

'Nobody's ever asked me that before,' he said. 'I'll have to find out.'

Brambling was still going through his ledger, page by page, in search of an answer, when I said goodbye and left him to it. I had decided to pay Greylag a surprise visit, so I strolled across the park with my sixpence in my pocket. It must have rained during the night because there were large puddles of water lying everywhere. I wondered vaguely how the weather affected Whimbrel's nocturnal activities. After all, he could hardly study the skies when there were great rain clouds blocking his view. I remembered that prior to the cabinet meeting he'd mentioned something about 'the astronomer's bane', but I hadn't really paid much attention. Presumably this was what he'd been referring to.

I approached the cake and entered by the postern door. Over the past few days I'd discovered that apart from the main door there were also three fire exits and a small side entrance. This led all the way to the orchestra pit via a tiled passage. Even before I opened the door I could hear music playing, and once I was inside the building it resounded ever more loudly. As I expected, the orchestra was playing a variation on the imperial anthem. I'd heard this one before and it was already my favourite: a piece of music in which the melody seemed to go round and round even more frequently than usual, as if it was somehow being constantly folded into itself. Greylag had previously explained to me that this particular variation was known as a fugue. Furthermore, each different treatment had its own designated number. The one I could hear at present, apparently, was the sixth in the sequence.

During my brief tenure the musicians had learnt not to bother rising to their feet every time I put in an appearance. I'd

41

made it clear that I preferred them to carry on as normal, and today was no exception. As I entered the pit, Greylag glanced in my direction, we exchanged nods and I headed straight for the podium. From somewhere or other he'd unearthed a proper conductor's baton for me to use. I found it where I'd left it last time, lying on top of the podium rail, and for the next twenty minutes I enjoyed 'leading' my orchestra through the sixth variation.

Eventually, though, I gave Greylag the signal to stop, and after another few bars the music ceased.

'Thank you, Greylag,' I said, stepping down from the podium. 'That was very good.'

'Yes, sir,' he replied.

'I've been meaning to ask you,' I continued. 'Is there any other music apart from the imperial anthem and its variations?'

'Well, we do have the other composers, sir. Which one would you like?'

'Who've you got?'

'All of them, sir.'

'All the famous ones?'

'Of course, sir.'

Greylag went to the antechamber and opened a cupboard, returning a minute later with a stack of manuscripts.

'Here we are, sir,' he said, and began leafing through the papers, one by one. 'We have the joyous composer, the innovative composer, the outlandish composer, the dreary composer, the child prodigy, the charlatan, the . . .'

'Just a second,' I said. 'Which one's the charlatan?'

Greylag handed me the manuscript and at once I recognised the name of the composer in question.

'Oh, I quite like his music,' I said. 'Why do you call him a charlatan?'

Greylag stood awkwardly before me, but said nothing.

'Come on,' I urged. 'Don't be shy.'

'Well, sir,' he said after a pause. 'In the humble opinion of the orchestra, he's a complete fake.'

As usual all the other musicians were sitting around us in silent rows, their instruments perched on their laps. I'd become accustomed to Greylag acting as their spokesman and the rest of them remaining mute. This last utterance, however, caused a low murmur of assent to pass through their ranks.

'A fake, eh?' I said. 'How do you mean exactly?'

'We consider his compositions to be laboured,' said Greylag. 'They lack any lightness of touch, which is the sure sign of a true artist. Take his first symphony, for example. We start off skipping through the flowery fields; then suddenly we're crawling through hell's cauldron; then we're back in the flowers again; then there's an angry bit; then a quiet bit; then another angry bit. None of it seems to have any proper meaning. As I said before, sir, a complete fake. Writing a symphony should be like constructing a universe. You can't simply make it up as you go along.'

After he'd reached his conclusion, Greylag reddened somewhat and bowed his head, perhaps thinking that he'd overstepped the mark a little.

I puffed out my cheeks. 'Well, Greylag,' I said, 'you obviously have very strong views on the subject.'

'Yes, sir,' he said quietly.

'And what about these variations?' I asked. 'Who composed them?'

'They're all ascribed to you, sir.'

'Me?' I said, astounded. 'How can I have composed them? I've only been here a week and a half!'

'As Principal Composer to the Imperial Court, sir, all new works are ascribed to you.'

'Yes, but who actually writes them?'

Once again Greylag appeared overcome by reticence, and once again I had to drag the answer out of him.

'Who writes them, Greylag?' I repeated.

'I do, sir.'

'Every one of them?'

'Yes, sir.'

'I see.'

For a minute I stood silently absorbing the implications of what I'd just heard. Then suddenly I was struck by a remarkable thought. Judging by the quality of his musicianship, Greylag had the ability to turn me into one of the greatest composers the court had ever seen. All I needed to do was look and learn, and bide my time.

'Was there anything else, sir?' enquired Greylag.

'Not for the moment,' I replied. 'Perhaps we should have another variation.'

'Very well, sir,' he said. 'Would you like to hear the seventh?'

'That will do nicely, Greylag, but I think we'll try something

44

slightly different today.' I handed him the baton and pointed towards the podium. 'You can conduct from up there for a change.'

'Thank you, sir,' said Greylag. 'I think you'll like this one. It goes at quite a gallop.'

The entire orchestra stirred with anticipation as Greylag headed for the podium and mounted the steps.

'All right, everyone,' he said, tapping the rail with his baton. 'This time I want to hear the hooves of the imperial cavalry!'

Yet again they launched headlong into the anthem, and now they were playing one of 'my' compositions! I watched and listened with pride as the music soared up into the highest corners of the auditorium. I could see plainly that the podium was the natural place for Greylag to be, and I determined to allow him a much freer hand in future.

This seventh variation definitely went at 'quite a gallop', and the theme had already come back round to the beginning when I noticed someone standing up at the rear of the hall, just along from the main doorway. The figure was half-concealed in the gloom, but after some moments I realised it was Wryneck. He appeared to be watching the proceedings intently, but the instant he saw me looking he turned and walked towards the door.

'Wryneck!' I called, but my voice was drowned out by the orchestra.

I signalled Greylag to carry on, and then walked swiftly up the centre aisle. By the time I reached the door and looked outside Wryneck was striding away across the park.

'Wryneck!'

Again there was no response, and he had soon disappeared into the distance. Inside the cake, the orchestra played on. Meanwhile, the trees rustled in the rising breeze. Another afternoon was fading towards twilight. For a few minutes I stood in the doorway pondering Wryneck's unheralded visit. I decided it was quite rude of him to leave without even acknowledging me, but after that I thought no more of it. The time had arrived for me to go on a certain errand.

During my earlier explorations of the royal quarter I had made an interesting find. Just around the corner from the Maypole I'd noticed a shop with the word HOBBY painted in large letters above its front window. This was no ordinary 'hobby' shop, however. Hobby was the name of its proprietor, and what it sold was all kinds of confectionery. The window was filled, row upon row, with neatly labelled jars of sweets.

I arrived about half past five and gazed through the leaded glass at yellow pear drops, pink marshmallows and golden sticks of barley sugar. There were sherbet fizzers, peppermints, liquorice comfits and the proprietor's very own dolly mixture. Further back I could see fruit pastilles, fondant creams, caramel fudge, everlasting toffee, coconut ice, butterscotch, choco-late nougat, hearts-of-violet, strawberry shrimps, bulls-eyes, broken rock, lemon crystals, jelly babies, rhubarb-and-custard, alphabet candies, black jacks and gunpowder lozenges. A small bell rang as I opened the door and entered the shop. Instantly I detected the scent of aniseed, vanilla, cinnamon and sarsapa-rilla. Yet more jars lined seemingly endless shelves. Outside, the sun was gradually sinking, and as it did the light appeared to refract through these colourful jars so that the whole shop was immersed in a soft, reddish gleam.

I was just peering at a jarful of 'lions and tigers' when suddenly I heard a voice behind me.

'Had a good look, have you, sir?'

I turned to see a man emerging from the dimness at the back of the shop. He was wearing a white linen coat.

'Yes, thank you,' I replied. 'I see you've got a very extensive range.'

'Indeed we have, sir. Indeed we have.'

'So I'd like to buy some of your wares.'

My comment evidently came as something of a surprise to the shopkeeper. He raised his eyebrows and gave me a quizzical look before moving behind the counter. This was equipped with a pair of scales.

'What can we do for you, sir?'

The way he addressed me as 'sir' was quite different from the subservient tone employed by Greylag. By contrast, this 'sir' was spoken with a sort of begrudging courtesy. In other words, I got the impression that he only called me 'sir' because it would be discourteous not to. Customers, apparently, were an inconvenience which he was obliged to tolerate. Nevertheless, I was much taken by the contents of his shop, so I made up my mind to ignore his unfortunate manner.

'To start with,' I said, 'I'd like some jelly babies and some sherbet fizzers.'

'Separate bags, sir?' enquired the shopkeeper.

'Oh no,' I said. 'Put them all together please.'

'As you wish, sir.'

He unscrewed the appropriate jars and tipped a few sweets on to the scales. Then he waited.

'Some lions and tigers,' I continued. 'Also, some rhubarb-and-custard, some hearts-of-violet, some liquorice comfits and some peppermint creams.'

Again he tipped out the required sweets.

'How much does that all come to?' I asked.

He placed a weight on the opposite scale. Then he added another. 'It comes to fivepence, sir.'

'Ah, good,' I said. 'Then I'll just have some of your dolly mixture to round it up to sixpence.'

'Round it up, sir?' said the shopkeeper.

'Yes.'

'But you're only allowed a pennyworth.'

'Why?'

'It's an imperial decree, sir, to stop people from being greedy.'

'But they're not for me,' I protested.

'Ho ho,' answered the shopkeeper. 'That's what they all say.'

'No, really,' I said. 'I'm Principal Composer to the Imperial Court.'

'I know exactly who you are, sir.'

'The sweets are for my musicians,' I explained. 'They've been working very hard lately and I want to reward them with a treat.'

The shopkeeper frowned.

'Well, sir,' he said, 'if you don't mind my saying so, I think that's a big mistake. Oh, I know you're only trying to be nice to them, but what you regard as an act of kindness they're sure to interpret as a sign of weakness. Believe me; I know what these serfs can be like.'

'Do you?'

'Yes, sir.'

The shopkeeper stood with his hands flat on the counter and a broad smile on his face. He was clearly very pleased with himself.

'All right then,' I said, after giving the situation a moment's thought. 'I'll just have a pennyworth.' I put my hand in my pocket and produced my stipendiary sixpence.

He shook his head.

'I'm very sorry, sir, but I can't take that.'

'Why not?' I queried. 'Haven't you got any change?'

'Yes, I have,' he said, 'but I can't just go dishing out pennies willy-nilly. Pennies are for commoners.'

'Oh,' I said, 'I see.'

I stood there clutching my sixpence in the palm of my hand. It was all I had, but I was quite unable to spend it.

'Tell you what, sir,' said the shopkeeper, 'how about a toffee apple on the house?'

5

On Wednesday afternoon at ten to three I rounded up
Whimbrel and Brambling, and we went over to the great
library. Smew was due to deliver one of his talks on the history
of the empire, and apart from anything else I was interested
to find out who would be there. The great library was an
impressive edifice with a huge pair of wooden doors at the
front. These doors remained wide open for long periods every
day, as if inviting people to come and see the vast collection
of books inside. We spent a few minutes admiring an apparently infinite maze of fully laden shelves; then we proceeded
to the reading room. This was an annexe at the west side of
the building, graced with a large bay window which allowed
the daylight to come flooding in. There were a good few
bookshelves here as well; also, some carefully placed tables
and chairs. Everything was arranged, it seemed, for the con-
venience of the reader.

Today, however, half a dozen extra chairs had been added
to accommodate Smew's listeners. These were positioned in

two rows of three. Before them was a small lectern. When we arrived Smew was standing with his back to us, staring out of the bay window as if completely lost in thought. It came as no surprise to see that Wryneck was already sitting in one of the front seats. Also present, immediately behind him, was Sanderling. There was no sign, though, of either Dotterel or Garganey. The clock had begun striking three when Brambling and Whimbrel slid into the other two seats in the back row. I sat down in the front row, at the opposite end to Wryneck. Then Smew turned and addressed us from the lectern.

'You'll be pleased to hear,' he began, 'that I am not a dates man. It makes no difference to me when such-and-such an event occurred. Such details are for the record books only, and have no relevance in the stream of history. Therefore, we will not be learning any dates during the course of this talk.'

From Wryneck there now came an appreciative chuckle, as though he was sharing some sort of 'in' joke with Smew. The rest of us were silent.

'Neither will I be listing any princes, kings or even emperors,' Smew continued. 'I am not concerned with naming names despite their undoubted achievements. Instead, I intend to talk today about the empire itself; about the process by which it came about; and about the factors which sustain it.'

While Smew spoke I found myself gazing at the walls that rose up around the bay window. Looking down at us from these heights were several portraits of previous emperors; but none, yet, of the latest incumbent. Smew stood below them at the lectern, having just revealed that they would not be included in his talk.

'So how does an empire begin?' he asked. 'Well, in our case it started with sailing ships. As we all know, the realm of Fallowfields lies on a western seaboard with many natural harbours and landing places. Consequently, our people since time immemorial have been masters of the deep. They built the finest vessels; they sailed and traded north and south along the coast; they cast their nets and brought home all manner of fish; and the more time they spent plying the waters, the broader their knowledge of ships and sailing came to be.'

Smew went on to describe how we swiftly attained maritime supremacy over our landlocked neighbours in the east. Hemmed in by swamps and forests, they were unable to reach the ocean without passing down our rivers and through our great ports. For this privilege they were required to pay 'ship money' which went directly into our coffers. Yet even when they finally left the harbour their seamanship was instantly exposed as being far inferior to ours. Smew told us a number of enjoyable tales about how our ships were often obliged to go and rescue theirs because they'd been blown off course; or because they'd simply lost their way. They were hopeless at navigation compared to us; there was no question of that. Furthermore, their ships had a marked tendency to sink without trace. Whenever we put to sea we invariably gained an advantage, one way or another, and this was all because we were better at sailing than anyone else.

'And because we were better at sailing,' announced Smew, 'we gradually came to believe that we were superior in all other respects as well. At some stage we began to use the title "Greater Fallowfields", rather than the more literal "Fallow Fields" of yore. "Greater" was a purely geographical term, of course, and originally appeared on maps; its purpose was to include the islands and inhabited sandbanks dotted along our coastline. Very soon, however, we started to take it as meaning "greater" as in "more important". The way was now open for us to declare ourselves an empire, which we duly did.'

Smew paused and glanced at his audience. He had been going for a good hour and the talk had certainly been absorbing. To my left, I realised for the first time that Wryneck was busy taking notes of the lecture. Now he stopped writing and waited with pen poised for Smew to resume. Someone in the seats behind me shuffled his feet restlessly. I guessed it was Whimbrel. All else remained quiet in the reading room. A few moments passed; then Smew turned towards the bay window and looked out.

'Nonetheless,' he said, still with his back turned, 'it should be emphasised that the empire was not established by force-of-arms. Such action would have been regarded as most improper. Instead, we strove merely to create benign "spheres of influence". Just beyond the border existed several small duchies and principalities who found it quite convenient to drift into our sway, especially as they were thereby exempt from paying "ship money". Other outlying territories were incorporated because they happened to share the same language. Hence, the "associated realms and dominions" began slowly to come into being. Meanwhile, in dealing with our larger neighbours, and those countries which were further removed, we chose to lead by example. We soon discovered that we could win people over by setting high standards in diplomacy, husbandry and good governance; in short, by showing them that our way of doing things was always the best. It was not long before the whole world wished only to emulate this illustrious empire of ours; and in the next talk I'll examine the subject in greater depth.'

Smew turned away from the window, and then stood stock still with a pained expression on his face. For a second I was unable to discern the cause of his disquiet, but when I looked around I saw that the seats behind me were all empty. It seemed the Chancellor of the Exchequer, the Astronomer Royal and the Comptroller for the Admiralty had all sneaked out before the end of the talk.

'That was shameful!' snapped Wryneck. He rose to his feet and began marching towards the door. 'I'm going to have a severe word with those three individuals!'

'Don't bother, Wryneck,' said Smew. 'If they weren't interested they weren't interested. It can't be helped.'

All the same, he was clearly disappointed and I had to admit I felt rather sorry for him.

'Well, if it's worth anything,' I said, 'I found the talk very interesting.'

'Did you really?' asked Smew.

'Of course,' I said. 'I'll definitely be attending the next one.'

'How kind,' he said. 'Thank you.'

Wryneck was still hovering nearby. Now he turned to me. 'Fond of history, are you?'

'Yes,' I replied. 'I do quite like it.'

'I see.'

'How about you?'

'Naturally, I'm interested in the history of the empire,' he said. 'It would be unthinkable not to be.'

'Indeed.'

Wryneck stared at me unblinkingly, but said nothing more. Meanwhile, Smew was beginning to perk up a little.

'Like some tea?' he enquired.

'Oh, thanks,' I said. 'That would be nice.'

'Lemon curd and toasted soldiers?'

'Sounds even better.'

'I'll see what I can do.'

Over by the doorway, a tasselled cord dangled from the ceiling. Smew pulled it and an instant later Shrike appeared. As usual he was wearing the full imperial livery.

'Ah, Shrike,' said Smew. 'Can we have tea for three please?'

'Here in the reading room, sir?'

'Of course.'

'Very good, sir.'

Shrike went off with his orders, while Smew led Wryneck and me over to the bay window. Situated here were some very comfortable chairs and a desk covered in books and papers. Smew asked us to sit down, and it quickly became evident that this was his own personal little corner. Through the window we could see a beautiful walled garden, and beyond it lay the royal palace. Some minutes later, Shrike arrived with the tea, as well as a huge plate of toasted soldiers and a pot of lemon curd. The three of us passed the next half hour in resplendent ease, and at last I felt I was sampling some of the perquisites of high office. Finally, at about five o'clock, the sun began to set over the palace, casting warm beams of light on Smew, Wryneck and myself.

'Marvellous,' uttered Smew. 'Absolutely marvellous.'

'Make the most of it,' I said. 'The clocks will be going back soon.'

'Ah, yes,' said Smew. 'I'd forgotten about the altering of the clocks. Why does that happen, by the way? I've never quite understood.'

'I'm not certain,' I answered, 'but I think it's to prepare the populace for the twelve-day feast; for all those long, dark evenings when the public houses are full to the brim.'

'You mean places like the Maypole?' said Smew.

'Yes.'

'I've heard it's a den of iniquity,' said Wryneck.

'You've never been inside then?'

'No, I haven't.'

'Nor me,' said Smew.

'Well,' I said, 'I propose to pay a visit one evening, so if anyone wishes to accompany me they're very welcome.'

'You'll excuse me if I say no,' murmured Wryneck, before pouring himself another cup of tea.

We were still basking in the glow of sunset when suddenly the door opened and in walked Garganey.

'Oh,' he said when he saw us. 'You're still here.'

'Naturally, we're still here,' said Smew.

'Then you'll forgive me if I sound selfish, gentlemen, but I was hoping to have the place to myself for a while. I intend to spend an hour studying our play.'

'That's very commendable,' remarked Smew. 'I'm impressed.'

'It's not a question of anyone being impressed,' countered Garganey. 'It's a question of doing something properly if it's going to be done at all.'

'I quite agree,' said Smew, 'and I dare say we'll all be on our way once the sun's gone down. Meanwhile, why don't you join us for some tea?'

'Thank you, no,' said Garganey. 'There isn't time.'

'Of course there's time,' said Smew. 'I insist.'

Smew quickly gave up his seat to Garganey and found another for himself. Garganey offered no further protest and sat down, although he was plainly reluctant to do so. Then Shrike was summoned and dispatched with another order for tea and toasted soldiers.

'Apologies for missing your talk,' said Garganey, 'but I've had a hectic day.'

'Anything serious?' Smew asked.

'It's difficult to know at this stage,' Garganey replied. 'My postmen seem to have some reservations about the changes I've been implementing. Do you remember we agreed that they were going to have their breakfast before they went out in the mornings?'

'As discussed in cabinet,' said Wryneck.

'Exactly,' said Garganey. 'It was discussed at the highest level, yet today I received a delegation of postmen who informed me that they weren't happy about having their breakfasts moved.'

'Really?'

'They said that such had been the blow to their morale it could only be detrimental to the postal service.'

At this moment Shrike returned with a heavily laden tray. As fresh supplies of tea and toast were dispensed, Garganey said nothing about the fact that we were being served by a liveried attendant in full imperial regalia. Perhaps his earlier misgivings had begun to subside. Or maybe he was simply too preoccupied with his own concerns to notice. Either way, he now lapsed temporarily into silence while Shrike poured out the tea.

'Why can't you just command your postmen to do as they're told?' suggested Wryneck at length.

'Because they're not serfs,' said Garganey. 'They're commoners.'

'I see.'

'Moreover, they're fully aware that the changes are only for a trial period and don't carry the full weight of an imperial edict.'

'In other words they're being awkward.'

'I don't really like to call it awkwardness,' said Garganey. 'After all, they're only trying to maintain what they see as a tradition, however archaic it might appear. We're talking about honourable men with unbending principles. Yet they also have ordinary desires. With this in mind I attempted to soften them up a little this afternoon, though I'm afraid my efforts were to no avail.'

'What happened?'

'I took the delegation along to the confectioner's shop and offered to buy them all a treat; but then that damned Hobby refused to accept my stipendiary sixpence. I felt most humiliated.'

'I don't doubt it,' said Smew.

'He even had the cheek to offer me a toffee apple in recompense.'

'Did you accept?' I asked.

'Certainly not,' said Garganey. 'The delegation had already taken their leave and I had to set off after them. Eventually, after much persuasion, they agreed to continue with the trial for the time being, but the situation remains unsatisfactory.'

'As you correctly pointed out,' said Wryneck, 'the full weight of an imperial edict would have been helpful.'

'Quite,' said Garganey.

While we'd been talking the sun had finally dipped behind the royal palace. Soon Shrike reappeared and cleared away the teacups. Then he started going around lighting the lamps.

'All right, Garganey,' said Smew, rising from his seat. 'I suppose you want some peace and quiet so you can get down to studying the play?'

'Yes, if nobody minds,' replied Garganey. 'I'd like to rehearse my role as king.'

'Temporary role,' said Wryneck.

'Of course,' said Garganey.

6

The next afternoon I visited the observatory and discovered
that Whimbrel had painted the word JUPITER across one of his
window frames.

'Why've you done that?' I asked.

'As a reminder,' he said.

'Yes, but Jupiter's not going to be in that window for ever,
is it?'

'Why not?' said Whimbrel. 'You told me all the stars were
fixed.'

'They're all fixed relative to one another, yes,' I said, 'but
Jupiter isn't a star; it's a planet. It's always on the move.'

'Well, it was there last night,' he retorted. 'I checked especially to make sure I had the correct window.'

'Yes, but it's only going to be there for a few weeks and
then it'll be gone.'

'What?' said Whimbrel with dismay. 'It took me all morning to paint those letters so neatly.'

'It does look neat,' I conceded, 'but I'm sorry to say you

were wasting your time. Nothing stands still in the universe. It's like a huge celestial clock with all the parts revolving.'

'Very well,' replied Whimbrel. 'If it's a clock I'll simply have to wait until Jupiter comes back round again.'

I gave a sigh.

'Look, Whimbrel,' I said, 'I really think you need to study these matters in more depth. When I said "clock" I actually meant "clocks within clocks". All the planets are on different orbits to us; Jupiter might not reappear in that particular window frame for months, or even years. Meanwhile, there'll be other planets with other names going by.'

'So how do I tell the planets from the stars?'

'Easy,' I said. 'Stars twinkle; planets don't.'

'Right.'

'There's only eight of them altogether and you can see some without your telescope.'

'Good,' said Whimbrel.

'Have you managed to get it working yet?'

'No, I haven't,' he said, 'but it so happens I was up on the roof tinkering with it just before you arrived. There's something I want to show you.'

He led the way up the iron ladder and on to the roof. The telescope stood jammed in its usual position.

'Look over there,' said Whimbrel, pointing to the east.

In that direction lay vast tracts of forest interspersed with open wilderness. The land was generally considered to be uninhabitable, and as such formed a natural boundary between the empire and her neighbours. The horizon was a blur of interminable greyness; but when I followed Whimbrel's gaze I thought I saw a plume of smoke rising up in the distance. It seemed to mark some sort of break in the terrain; hardly more than a vague line; barely discernible.

'What do you think that is?' I asked.

'I don't know,' said Whimbrel. 'I've been up here a few times recently. Sometimes I've seen smoke; sometimes I haven't.'

'Maybe some foresters have headed out there to give it a try,' I suggested. 'I know there've been several attempts in the past, but they've always returned saying it's too far away to be profitable.'

'You could be right,' said Whimbrel. 'All the nearby forests were used up during the great days of shipbuilding.'

'Pity that telescope of yours is out of action. Otherwise we could see much more clearly.'

Again we peered into the distance, but by now the smoke had begun to drift away. After a minute, however, another plume rose up. This was perhaps slightly nearer than before, though in truth it was very difficult to distinguish anything in the pervading murk. The more we looked, the less we were able to see, until eventually we gave up even trying.

'Come on, Whimbrel,' I said. 'It's cold up here; let's go back inside.'

'Yes, it is cold, isn't it?' he agreed. 'Autumn is certainly with us now.'

'I expect they've got a nice log fire in the Maypole.'

'That's exactly what I was going to say. I'm up here some

evenings and I see all the lights blazing and I think of that place. It looks so warm and inviting from the outside.'

We clambered back down the iron ladder.

'Tell you what,' I said. 'Do you fancy going there tonight?'

'The Maypole?'

'Yes.'

'Oh, I don't know,' said Whimbrel. 'According to Sanderling they employ a bevy of dancing girls.'

'Even better,' I rejoined. 'He's been there, has he?'

'No.'

'Well, we could invite him along too.'

'Are we allowed though?' Whimbrel asked.

'Of course we're allowed!' I said. 'We're officers-of-state; we can do whatever we like.'

'I must admit I've always found the prospect quite attractive.'

'Right, then, that's decided. I'll see you later, and if Sanderling wants to come as well, the more the merrier!'

I left Whimbrel pondering what to wear and headed across the park. In the past few days I'd made up my mind to allow the orchestra to have the cake to themselves in the evenings; I thought that this was the least I could do since they plainly had nowhere else to go. Dusk was only just approaching, however, so there was still plenty of time for me to call in and see what they were up to. I entered through the main door and imme-diately saw Greylag conducting once again from the podium. Strictly speaking this should have been regarded as an act of gross insubordination; after all, Greylag was only a serf, despite his undoubted musical talents. The podium was supposed to be out of bounds unless he received express permission. Recently, though, Greylag and I had come to an understanding whereby he was allowed to occupy the podium during practice sessions. I'd realised that he was much better able to carry out his work from this position; and that therefore in the long term it could only be to my advantage. Accordingly, the orchestra kept on going as I strode down the centre aisle and joined them in the pit.

What was difficult to tolerate, on the other hand, was the music itself. To be frank it was quite terrible: a wild, rampaging din that might be heard at some fiendish orgy. Furthermore, it was so loud it was deafening. Only when a particular phrase was repeated did it occur to me that I was listening to the imperial anthem being played at breakneck speed! I allowed Greylag to continue for a few more bars; then I raised my hand and within moments the racket ceased.

'What on earth's going on?' I demanded.

'I'm very sorry if it offended your ears, sir,' replied Greylag, 'but the piece is a useful means for exercising the orchestra.'

'Is it really necessary?'

'I'm afraid so, sir,' he said. 'We've been rather under-stretched of late.'

'You mean unchallenged?'

'Yes, sir.'

'I see.'

Greylag remained standing on the podium with this vast and accomplished, yet clearly unfulfilled, orchestra gathered all around him. Meanwhile, an idea that had been developing in the back of my mind gradually came to fruition. The moment was waiting to be seized.

I ordered Greylag to dismiss the musicians for the evening. They were soon packing away their instruments; then I sat him down and explained what I wanted to do.

'To coincide with the twelve-day feast,' I began, 'the cabinet has decided to present a courtly entertainment in the form of a play. I won't bother telling you the title because you probably won't have heard of it, but I'd like the orchestra to provide an overture which conveys the sense of turbulence, menace and impending doom that characterises the work. It will require elements suggesting nocturnal subterfuge, unnamed peril and grim descent, as well as the more obvious effects: wailing harbingers, howling winds, screeching owls, trumpet blasts, bells chiming, storms raging and cocks crowing.'

While I'd been talking I had hardly glanced at Greylag, but when finally I looked him in the face I saw that his eyes were glistening. He was paying the closest attention to my words, yet at the same time he appeared to be deep in thought, as if he was already plotting the course of the composition I'd requested.

'What do you think, Greylag?' I asked.

For a few seconds he seemed unable to reply. He was hardly even breathing and continued to just sit there with a faraway look in his eyes. Then at last he snapped out of it.

'Yes, sir,' he stammered. 'We can do it, and we can start at once!'

He rose to his feet and began pacing about with his hands clasped together.

'Yes, yes,' he continued, talking mostly to himself. 'We can have oboes. There must be oboes in the beginning, playing very faintly at first. Then the horns . . .'

Greylag broke off when he saw me staring at him.

'Go on,' I said. 'I'm listening.'

He came and stood before me. 'I'm sorry to get so carried away, sir, but such an opportunity hasn't come my way before. I promise I will do everything to make this the greatest piece of music you have ever heard.'

'I'm very glad to hear it, Greylag,' I said. 'So I can leave you to it, can I?'

'Yes, indeed, sir. Thank you, sir.'

'No, Greylag,' I said. 'It's me who should be thanking you.'

By the time I left the cake Greylag had recalled all the musicians and was addressing them from the podium. Outside, darkness had fallen. I wandered back across the park feeling most content. Greylag had promised me the greatest piece of music I'd ever heard, and I was determined to hold him to it. Tonight, however, the unknown pleasures of the Maypole awaited.

When I reached the observatory I found the door wide open. I could hear voices above, so quietly I mounted the spiral staircase. Whimbrel, it seemed, was giving Sanderling a guided tour. I listened with interest.

'Now in this window,' Whimbrel announced, 'we have Jupiter. The most majestic of celestial bodies, I'm sure you'll agree.'

'Hmm hmm,' said Sanderling.

'Obviously this particular display won't last long,' Whimbrel continued. 'Within only a few weeks Jupiter will be moving away on a separate orbit. Such are the motions of the heavens.'

I concluded that Whimbrel must have got down to studying his subject more thoroughly. I also realised that I could not carry on lurking in the shadows, so I clanged my feet on the iron stairway to make my presence known.

'Ah, there you are,' said Whimbrel when I reached the top. 'We've been waiting for you to arrive.'

'Good evening,' said Sanderling.

'Good evening,' I replied.

'I was just telling Sanderling about Jupiter,' Whimbrel informed me. 'Needless to say, it would look even better if we could use the telescope.'

'Doesn't yours work then?' enquired Sanderling.

'No,' said Whimbrel. 'It's jammed.'

'That's a shame.'

'I don't suppose you've got any spare telescopes over at the admiralty?'

'I'm afraid not,' said Sanderling.

'Oh.'

'We haven't got any ships either.'

'What!' exclaimed Whimbrel. 'You must have.'

'I can assure you we haven't.'

'I thought the whole empire was built on ships.'

'Maybe it was,' said Sanderling, 'but there aren't any now.'

'What do you do all day then?' I asked.

'Nothing much,' he said. 'I was thinking of learning about navigation but apparently you can't get started unless you know where north is.'

'Well,' I said, 'Whimbrel can show you how to find that.'

'Can I?' said Whimbrel. 'Oh, yes, north. Sorry. Follow me.'

He led Sanderling to one of the windows opposite and then explained in very precise terms exactly how to locate the Pole Star.

'That was very good,' I said, when he'd finished. 'I'm impressed.'

'I'm suddenly finding astronomy much more interesting,' Whimbrel answered, 'and I've decided I'm going to the library to read about it properly.'

'Even if Smew's there?' said Sanderling.

'Of course,' said Whimbrel. 'I'm an officer-of-state. I can go there whenever I like.'

'You're coming to Smew's next history talk as well,' I added.

'Am I?'

'Yes,' I said. 'You're going to sit next to me and not sneak out before the end.'

'What about me?' said Sanderling.

'I don't know,' I replied. 'You only seem interested in finding out about dancing girls.'

'Well, someone has to,' he said. 'Talking of which, aren't we supposed to be visiting the Maypole?'

Without further discussion the three of us buttoned our dandy coats and headed out into the night. A few minutes later, when we walked past the cake, I was pleased to hear the faint sound of instruments being tuned.

'Your musicians seem to be hard at work,' remarked Whimbrel.

'Oh, yes,' I said. 'They never rest.'

Our arrival at the Maypole was met by the usual din of laughter, songs and glasses tinkling. We looked at one another for a long moment; then I pushed open the door and we went inside. We found the place busy but not too crowded. Seated around the tables and in alcoves were an assortment of commoners. One or two of them glanced in our direction as we entered but the majority took no notice, which I had to admit came as a slight relief. There was, as I had imagined, a huge log fire blazing in the hearth; also a dartboard; and over in one corner a number of off-duty postmen were enjoying a noisy game of dominoes. I knew they were postmen by their familiar scarlet and black uniforms. I wondered vaguely how they managed to stay up late at night carousing when they had to get up so early in the morning; but then I decided that they probably caught up with their sleep in the afternoons.

Opposite the door was a counter lined with hand-pumps; behind it stood the publican. He was polishing glasses very slowly, one by one, and placing them upside down on a shelf.

'Evening, gentlemen,' he said, as we approached.

'Evening,' I replied, before glancing at the other two. 'What are we having? Beer?'

'I've only got beer,' said the publican.

'Oh, right,' I said. 'Three beers then, please.'

70

'Allow me,' said Whimbrel. With a flourish he produced a bright sixpence from his pocket and laid it on the counter.

The publican peered down at the coin. 'The beer's a penny a pint,' he announced.

'Fine,' Whimbrel answered.

'That's a sixpenny piece you've got there.'

'Yes, well, I'm sure you must have plenty of change.'

'On the contrary,' said the publican. He turned to his till and pressed the 'no sale' key. The drawer sprang open to reveal that it was completely empty.

'Been a quiet night?' I asked.

'Not really,' he said. 'It's about average.'

'Oh.'

'Excuse me for a second, will you?'

Underneath one of the hand-pumps, a glass of beer was waiting to be made up to a full pint. The publican spent the next few moments carefully topping it off. Then he placed the glass on the counter and nodded at one of the postmen, who came over and took it without uttering a word.

I was beginning to feel quite thirsty. I watched as the postman rejoined his companions and they all raised their glasses in a raucous toast. The dominoes continued to clatter. Meanwhile, the publican went around the tables collecting empty glasses from customers who all seemed to have full ones close at hand. Finally, he resumed his station behind the counter.

'So you can't change a sixpence?' enquired Whimbrel.

'I'm afraid not,' said the publican.

'In that case we'll have six pints all at once. I expect the three of us can manage two pints apiece.'

'That's not allowed,' said the publican. 'You can only have a fresh pint when you've finished the last one.'

'By imperial decree?' I ventured.

'Correct.'

'What about the commoners?'

'What about them?'

'They've all got pints lined up,' I pointed out. 'How do they pay?'

The publican drew us closer and spoke in a lowered voice. 'Most of them haven't got a penny to their name,' he said. 'They get all their beer on tick.'

'Then the solution is obvious,' said Sanderling. 'We'll have ours on tick as well. Just so long as you don't mind, that is.'

'Certainly I don't mind,' replied the publican. 'You can run a slate if you wish but it won't look very good, will it?'

Whimbrel, Sanderling and I gazed at one another in dismay. The publican was right, of course. We were officers-of-state. It would have been quite unacceptable for us to receive our drinks on tick, especially in front of all these commoners.

It struck me that the publican had a similar manner to the confectioner, though I noticed he called none of us 'sir'. Now he stood with his hands flat on the counter and a broad smile on his face. He was clearly very pleased with himself.

'What are we going to do?' murmured Sanderling. He was suddenly sounding desperate.

'All I can suggest is that we go back to the observatory for a nightcap,' said Whimbrel.

Sanderling's face lit up in an instant. 'That's a relief,' he said. 'For a minute I thought we were destined for a "dry" evening.'

'No, no,' said Whimbrel. 'I've got a bottle or two we can open.'

'Right,' I said. 'That's decided then.'

Politely we thanked the publican for his hospitality.

'My pleasure,' he said, as we made for the door. 'Goodnight.'

'Goodnight,' we all chorused.

Once we got outside Sanderling said, 'Shame there weren't any dancing girls. We must have chosen the wrong evening.'

'Definitely the wrong evening,' I agreed.

The three of us trudged towards the park. The moon had risen but the sky was black.

'Listen,' said Whimbrel.

We stopped and listened. For a moment all was quiet. Then in the distance we heard a prolonged roll of thunder.

'Did that come from the east?' asked Sanderling.

'Don't know,' I said. 'You tell me.'

7

As the clock struck ten, Smew opened the register.

'Let us begin,' he said, taking up his pencil. 'Chancellor of the Exchequer?'

'Present,' said Brambling.

'Postmaster General?'

'Present,' said Garganey.

'Astronomer Royal?'

'Present,' said Whimbrel.

'Comptroller for the Admiralty?'

'Present,' said Sanderling.

'Surveyor of the Imperial Works?'

'Present,' said Dotterel.

'Pellitory-of-the-Wall?'

'Present,' said Wryneck.

'Principal Composer to the Imperial Court?'

'Present,' I said.

'His Exalted Highness, the Majestic Emperor of the Realms, Dominions, Colonies and Commonwealth of Greater Fallowfields?'

There was no response.

'Absent,' said Smew.

I couldn't see whether he put a cross or a tick in the register, because once again he was holding it tilted slightly towards him.

'Oh, that reminds me,' said Wryneck. 'We've received a letter from the emperor.'

From his inside pocket he produced an envelope. It was addressed to the cabinet and bore the imperial seal.

'Before we open it can I have a look at the postmark?' said Garganey.

'Certainly,' said Wryneck.

He handed the envelope across the table and Garganey examined it closely.

'Interesting,' he said. 'This has taken four days to arrive, yet it was only posted around the corner.'

'How do you know?' asked Smew.

'Postmarks vary throughout the empire,' Garganey explained. 'This was posted here in the royal quarter.'

'So where's it been in the meantime?'

'Good question,' said Garganey. 'Clearly my efficiency measures are taking a while to work their way through the system. All the same, I intend to persevere until I see some improvement.'

'At least this tells us the emperor is near at hand,' said Whimbrel.

'Was there ever a suggestion he wasn't?' enquired Wryneck.

'Not that I've heard.'

'What did you mean then?'

'Just . . .'

'His Majesty is absent from cabinet,' interrupted Smew, 'which is all we need to know. Any further conjecture is unnecessary.'

An awkward silence followed during which Garganey opened the envelope. Inside was an ornate card, which he passed around for each of us to see. It read:

THE EMPEROR OF GREATER FALLOWFIELDS

HEREBY EXPRESSES HIS WISH FOR A

COURTLY ENTERTAINMENT

TO MARK THE OCCASION

OF THE

TWELVE–DAY FEAST.

'There we are,' said Smew. 'I thought we'd receive an official reminder eventually.'

'Rather a low-key request,' I observed. 'It certainly lacks the grand tone of previous communications.'

'Nevertheless, it carries the same weight as any other imperial edict,' said Wryneck.

'Indeed,' said Smew. 'Now we'd better get on. Can we all turn to page forty-three in our textbooks?'

Everybody helped themselves from the stack of books in the centre of the table. There still weren't enough to go around, however, so again I had to share with Whimbrel.

'Now if I remember rightly,' resumed Smew, 'Sanderling was the murderer, Whimbrel the ghost and Garganey the king. I'll be the lady and the rest of you are the noble guests. Decide amongst yourselves who's going to be who and then we can begin.'

Dotterel, Brambling, Wryneck and I quickly shared out the remaining roles.

Meanwhile, Garganey rose from his seat and started walking around the table in a very self-conscious manner.

'A final note,' said Smew. 'Don't forget that the king is the only person who can't see the ghost. All right, Whimbrel, proceed when you're ready.'

'Proceed where?' Whimbrel asked.

'You're supposed to sit down.'

'I'm sitting down already.'

'No,' said Smew, 'you have to enter the room and sit in the king's place.'

'Oh,' said Whimbrel, 'right.'

He got up, went out of the room, then came back and sat down on Garganey's empty chair. In the meantime, Garganey continued to walk around the table. When nobody spoke he walked round again.

'Come on, someone,' urged Smew.

'Sorry,' said Brambling. 'I missed my cue. Please Your Highness to grace us with your company?'

'The table's full,' said Garganey.

'Here's a place reserved, sir,' said Dotterel.

'Where?' said Garganey.

'Here, my good lord,' said Dotterel. 'What is it that moves Your Highness?'

'Which of you have done this?' said Garganey.

'Done what?' said Dotterel.

'That's my line, actually,' said Wryneck, 'and you said it wrong.'

'I'm fully aware whose line it is,' replied Dotterel. 'I'm just asking what's been done?'

'Well, haven't you read the play?' asked Smew.

'Of course I have.'

'Then you must know about the murder.'

'Yes,' said Dotterel, 'and so does the king.'

'Your point being?'

'My point being that you said the king is the only person who can't see the ghost.'

'Correct,' said Smew.

'So if he can't see the ghost why does he ask who's done it?'

'Maybe I'm sitting in the wrong seat?' suggested Whimbrel.

'No, I don't think so,' said Dotterel.

Smew gave a sigh. 'Perhaps we should all have a discussion about the meaning of the play,' he said. 'Just to ensure we're all reading from the same page, so to speak.'

'I agree,' said Garganey, sitting down in Whimbrel's place.

'That's settled then,' said Wryneck.

There was a brief hiatus in the conversation while everybody looked through their texts.

Then Smew said, 'All right, does anyone want to tell us what this play's about?'

'Well, basically,' said Brambling, 'it's about this nobleman who's told by the oracles that he'll be king; and that his friend, who's also a nobleman, won't.'

Smew frowned.

'A brief but fairly accurate summary as far as it goes,' he announced, 'but really I was referring to the broader meaning of the play.'

'Oh,' said Brambling, 'sorry.'

'It's an example of the feudal system in perfect working order,' said Wryneck, 'until someone tampers with it.'

'Very concise,' said Smew. 'Yes, to operate properly a feudal kingdom depends on obedience, trust, honour and duty. Here we have a generous king surrounded by his loyal noblemen and all appears to be well. The natural order is upset, however, by ambition, treason and murder. You'll also notice that the play lacks any kind of sub-plot. There are no trivial sideshows or distractions. All is cast in desolate shade. The entire five acts are weighed down with the consequences of treachery. Even the murderers mistrust one another.'

We sat in silence around the table, each of us pondering Smew's stark description. Through the windows I could see dark clouds approaching. There'd been rain overnight and now, it seemed, it was going to rain again. The hands of the clock had almost reached eleven. This meant that the meeting would soon be over.

'By the way,' I said, 'I've taken the liberty of commissioning some music to accompany the play.'

'Really?' said Smew. 'So we can look forward to hearing it portrayed in abstract symphonic terms?'

'Hopefully,' I replied.

'Or will it be simply a variation on the imperial anthem?' enquired Wryneck.

'Certainly not,' I said. 'What are you implying?'

'I'm implying nothing,' said Wryneck, 'but you may wish to know that altering the imperial anthem is officially regarded as an act of treason.'

'Oh,' I said. 'I had no idea.'

'I've been studying the public records,' said Wryneck. 'They make very interesting reading.' He now turned to Garganey. 'It is also treasonous to interfere with the imperial postal service.'

'Even to make improvements?' said Garganey.

'I'm afraid so,' replied Wryneck. 'I'm only telling you this for your own good, you understand.'

'Thank you,' said Garganey, 'and what's your function exactly?'

'I'm Pellitory-of-the-Wall,' said Wryneck. 'The name speaks for itself.'

8

When the rain came down, Whimbrel was unable to see the stars. Instead, he spent the evening in the observatory studying his charts. He'd been in the library all afternoon reading about astronomy and at last he appeared to be making some progress. I watched as he worked with ruler and compasses, making calculations and writing the results on his notepad. Eventually, though, he decided he'd learned enough for one day.

'I meant to tell you,' he said. 'Sanderling has heard a rumour.'

'Not another bevy of dancing girls?'

'No, no,' said Whimbrel, 'nothing like that. Apparently a troupe of strolling players arrived at the imperial gates yesterday morning and asked to be allowed into the royal quarter.'

'Why did they have to ask?' I said. 'Those gates are purely ceremonial. They're never closed.'

'Well, you know what actors are like,' said Whimbrel, 'always trying to seek attention.'

'Yes, I suppose so.'

'Sanderling says they've taken lodgings at the Maypole.'

'How did they manage that?' I demanded. 'We couldn't even get served a glass of beer.'

'Perhaps they're singing for their supper,' suggested Whimbrel. 'They can't have any money: they come from outside the empire.'

'Do they indeed?'

'According to the rumour, they've been travelling for weeks.'

'So they must have been caught in all that rain last night?'

'Probably, yes,' said Whimbrel.

This was a most unusual turn of events. Strangers from abroad rarely visited the heart of the empire, and I wondered what sort of life they lived. Then again, a rumour was only a rumour. I'd believe it when I saw these 'strolling players' for myself, and not a moment sooner.

'I've got some news too,' I said. 'Brambling maintains that we don't get another sixpence until we've spent the last one.'

'Really?' said Whimbrel.

'He's trawled all through his ledger and found the appropriate entry.'

'Well, my sixpence remains stubbornly unspent.'

'Mine too,' I said. 'In fact, I mentioned it to Brambling.'

'What did he say?'

'He told me we were lucky to get sixpence when the postmen only earn a penny a day.'

'That doesn't make sense.'

'No,' I agreed, 'I don't think Brambling knows very much about money.'

'Well, he is Chancellor of the Exchequer,' said Whimbrel. 'He's obviously perfect for the job.'

'Quite.'

For some reason I took my stipendiary sixpence from my pocket and began examining it closely. On one side was the head of a long-forgotten emperor; on the other was the image of a ship under full sail.

'Surprising, isn't it?' Whimbrel remarked. 'There seems to be hardly any coinage in circulation. I haven't laid eyes on a penny for weeks, let alone shillings or half-crowns; all I've seen are a few sixpences.'

'I suppose it could be argued,' I said, 'that a feudal society requires very little cash to keep going. Maybe a handful of coins are needed here and there, just to lubricate the wheels, but beyond that it probably suits the empire to keep everyone a bit "short"; to keep them down, as it were, so that nobody tries to get above themselves.'

Whimbrel stared at me in silence.

'What?' I asked.

'I really think you should be careful when you criticise the empire,' he replied. 'It may only be a casual observation but you never know who could be listening.'

'Don't tell me you believe all that nonsense about treason?'

'Well, you heard what Wryneck said.'

'Take no notice of Wryneck!' I snapped. 'He only raised the matter because he's got nothing better to do!'

'Yes,' conceded Whimbrel, 'he does appear to have rather a lot of spare time on his hands.'

'Besides,' I added, 'this is a thoroughly benign empire. It's all jumbled and disorganised; we have a vast hierarchy with serfs at the bottom and the emperor at the top, but in between there exists a pecking order that's vague and unfathomable to say the least; shopkeepers, publicans and postmen happily inconvenience officers-of-state whenever it takes their fancy; we have no police force; no army or navy; no tax collectors; and, finally, the emperor doesn't even bother to turn up for cabinet meetings.'

'Hmm, I see what you mean,' said Whimbrel. 'Treason would be pointless.'

'Exactly,' I said. 'There's no tyranny to overthrow.'

9

When I approached the cake I heard music playing in such plangent tones that for an instant I was stopped in my tracks. Had some tragedy occurred, I wondered, of which I was yet to be informed? It was certainly a day for such thoughts. Dark clouds were blowing in from the east on a wild and bitter wind, while all the trees rustled with their dead leaves.

The playing stopped. I waited and listened and after a time it resumed again. Now I could hear the plaintive sound of a lone oboe. It reminded me of a despondent cry in some remote region far beyond my reach.

I was almost tempted to turn back and leave Greylag to continue his work uninterrupted; he was obviously making excellent progress with the overture. I decided, however, that as Principal Composer I should at least show my face occasionally. Therefore, I opened the postern door and went in.

The lone oboe had now been joined by several others, and gradually they built on the theme he had been developing. I arrived in the orchestra pit just as they embarked on a shrill rampage that took them into battle with the piccolos and flutes. Moments later the trumpets appeared as if to separate the squabbling woodwind. Then Greylag noticed me and brought them all to a halt.

'Carry on, if you like, Greylag,' I said. 'It sounds marvellous.'

'Beg your pardon, sir,' he replied, 'but could you possibly listen to a particular section we've been practising, to tell me if you think it worthy of inclusion?'

'Of course, Greylag,' I said. 'I am always at your service.'

My ill-chosen words caused Greylag to redden slightly, but he quickly recovered and turned to the orchestra. As usual, the musicians had been sitting in silent rows awaiting their instructions. I noticed that they had handwritten scores on their music stands; and that these scores already ran to several dozen pages. On Greylag's orders they started leafing through to a certain point. Then, at last, they were ready to begin playing.

The music this time was different again. I recognised the same melody from the original theme, but now the entire brass section was on the march. When all the lower strings abruptly entered the fray I knew Greylag was building up to something. Cleverly, though, he allowed the whole orchestra to fade suddenly into nothingness. I now expected some sort of crescendo, but instead there appeared a distant horn which played half a phrase from the first theme. The notes were slightly discordant and it seemed like a mistake;

yet actually it was a carefully laid trap because *then* with a mighty crash came the crescendo!! The trap had been sprung!! I shuddered as my ninety-eight musicians drove onwards, soaring up to greater and greater heights, then plunging down to new depths.

I was willing to listen to more of this, but without warning the orchestra ceased playing.

Greylag turned and looked at me enquiringly.

'Well, well, Greylag,' I said. 'That was quite outstanding.'

'Thank you, sir.'

'What was that trick you pulled with the horn?'

'It's known as a "mort", sir,' Greylag replied. 'The call sounded by huntsmen to signify a kill.'

'Oh,' I said. 'I see.'

'May I take it that you approve then, sir?'

'Yes, yes, without a doubt. You can do whatever you think is right. In fact, feel free to depart from the usual rules and conventions. Develop your themes in any direction you choose.'

'Yes, sir. Thank you, sir.'

'By the way, when do you think you'll be finished?'

'I don't know, sir,' said Greylag. 'It seems to me that I'm only just beginning.'

'But you'll be ready in time for the twelve-day feast?'

'I'll do my best, sir. We're working all hours as it is.'

'Oh yes,' I said. 'I've observed the burning of the midnight lamp.'

I'd have liked to have been able to award Greylag and the orchestra a day off in recognition of their valiant efforts, but unfortunately this was beyond my gift. Furthermore, the constraints of time were pressing. The year was rolling steadily towards its close, and it was imperative that the overture was completed as soon as possible. With this in mind I decided to give Greylag as much praise and encouragement as I could, and then leave him to his own devices. For his part, he seemed so absorbed with his creation that the hours spent were not begrudged. As I left the cake he was already issuing new instructions to the musicians, who in their turn appeared similarly tireless.

I went outside and started walking across the park. As usual after hearing Greylag's music I felt uplifted, as if the cares of the day had been erased. The dark clouds had passed overhead, the wind had eased and all felt peaceful.

However, this did not stop me from being surprised by the sight of a man standing beneath the branches of a tree. He stood perfectly still in a very unusual pose that reminded me of a statue. After half a minute he changed to another position, and thereafter remained motionless.

He was wearing a magnificent crimson coat, but as I drew near I realised that it was a very poor fit. It was plainly one size too small for him. When he saw me he relaxed his pose.

'Good afternoon, sir,' he said.

This was a different 'sir' to those varieties spoken by Greylag or Hobby, being neither subservient nor falsely courteous. The delivery on this occasion was grand and self-possessed. Apparently I was being addressed as an equal, though the fellow was clearly some kind of vagabond.

I eyed him warily.

'Apologies for our appearance,' he said. 'We were caught in a downpour a few nights ago and our cherished coat has shrunk.'

'Why do you wear a coat like that anyway?' I enquired.

'You mean why do we dress in borrowed robes?'

'Yes, I suppose I do.'

'Because of whom we are, sir.'

'Well, who are you?'

'Gallinule,' he announced. 'Actor par excellence.'

The penny dropped at last. The strolling players! So the rumour was true after all.

'Gallinule?' I said. 'Are you famous then?'

'We have a circle of admirers,' he replied, 'although we are better known by our professional name.'

'Which is?'

'We are the Player King, sir. We specialise in all the royal roles: good kings, bad kings, kings in exile, deposed kings, begetters of kings, murdered kings, warrior kings, pretenders, tyrants, despots and usurpers.'

'Pleased to meet you,' I said. 'I'm Principal Composer to the Imperial Court.'

'We know exactly who you are, sir,' replied Gallinule.

'Ah.'

'Our troupe consists of eight players,' he added, 'and we are lodging at the Maypole if you'd care to drop by one evening.'

'I'll bear it in mind,' I promised.

We said goodbye and he struck another pose which I took to be a sort of salute. He was still standing in the same position when I looked back a while later, but I soon forgot about him and made my way towards the great library. It was time for another of Smew's talks. I had arranged to meet Whimbrel at the door, and I was pleased to see that he had kept the appointment. He'd even taken the trouble of bringing along his notepad. We went into the reading room and discovered that Garganey and Wryneck were also present; but there was no sign of Brambling, Dotterel or Sanderling.

'Never mind,' said Smew. 'I'm grateful to those who are here.'

All the chairs were laid out in readiness for the talk and now it was simply a matter of deciding where to sit. I made sure Whimbrel was next to me so that he couldn't misbehave. Wryneck joined us in the same row, while Garganey chose a seat slightly apart from the rest. Meanwhile, Smew took up position behind his lectern.

'When,' he began, 'did marmalade change from orange to quince?'

It was an unusual question and I have to confess I did not know the answer. Fortunately, this was merely Smew's way of introducing his talk. He went on to remind us of how the Empire of Greater Fallowfields had become a model of good governance; how we had established spheres of influence; and how the associated realms and dominions had striven to emu-late our ways.

'They quickly realised,' said Smew, 'that to be properly part of the empire they needed to become like us. This in turn required us to set an example, which we duly did by producing the Fallowfieldsman. He was the epitome of all we stood for. Wherever he travelled in the world, the Fallowfieldsman could always be told by his accent, his manners and his temperament. He frowned on uncouth practices but was never outspoken. When he went abroad he took with him the imperial flag, and this came to be widely recognised as a symbol of his natural authority over others; moreover, it was the only flag that could be flown upside down without anybody noticing. Such a remarkable fact was a source of great national pride, as was his steadfast determination never to learn a foreign language. This was considered quite unnecessary because any foreigner worth his salt would learn to speak like the Fallowfieldsman.'

The door opened and Gallinule came into the reading room. He glanced briefly at the little group assembled around Smew, nodded politely in our direction, then proceeded to wander along the rows of bookshelves examining odd titles here and there. He did all this in perfect silence before finally disappearing behind the furthest shelf. He failed to re-emerge.

Meanwhile, Smew continued his talk.

'For many years we carried on in the same way,' he said, 'and the associated realms and dominions became more and more obsequious. Accordingly, we tended to regard them as mere vassal states. We sailed to the south, exchanged a few worthless trinkets, and returned home with all their oranges.

We sailed to the north and helped ourselves to the best of their fish. In other words, we took full advantage of our sea-going skills. By this time we literally ruled the waves. We even claimed the prime meridian of longitude for ourselves, building an observatory especially to mark the spot, as Whimbrel here will no doubt verify.'

Smew paused and gave Whimbrel a quizzical look. This was met by an expression of utter bafflement from Whimbrel.

'Well, Whimbrel?' said Smew.

'Oh, yes, yes, of course,' Whimbrel eventually managed. 'The prime meridian of longitude. Yes.'

Smew gave him a penetrating stare before resuming his talk once again.

'It was at this stage,' he said, 'that some of our sailors began to venture due west, across the wider ocean. They said they were going to seek their fortunes, but they never came back. More sailors followed and they also failed to return. This was taken as evidence that there was nothing in the west except the prospect of shipwreck. Such a conclusion should have spelt an end to further exploits. It certainly reinforced our belief that we were at the centre of civilisation and that everywhere else verged on wilderness. At the same time, however, we knew we were the only people capable of sailing into the west. The implied challenge was unavoidable. Therefore, we continued sending out more and more of these so-called adventurers, even though they were never seen again. The consequences of such a policy were slow to reveal themselves, but gradually the empire became depleted both of ships and of the mariners to sail them. Which returns us to my original question: when did marmalade change from orange to quince?'

Smew ceased talking and surveyed his audience, as if waiting for an answer.

'When there were no ships left at all?' I offered.

'Correct,' said Smew, with a note of triumph, 'when there were no ships left at all.'

He took a small bow and to my surprise a round of applause broke out behind me. Glancing around I discovered that sometime during the talk Gallinule had slipped into the back row of seats. I must have been so engrossed with Smew's exposition that I failed to notice.

'Very, very interesting,' said Gallinule. 'Thank you.'

He quickly went forward and introduced himself to Smew. The pair of them seemed to hit it off at once, and not long afterwards Gallinule was being invited to tea in the large bay window. The invitation also included Wryneck, but not Garganey, Whimbrel or me. We watched as Shrike was summoned and dispatched again with an order for lemon curd and toasted soldiers.

'Damned rude,' muttered Garganey, before heading swiftly towards the door.

Then Whimbrel turned to me and asked, 'What did all that have to do with quince?'

I explained that there were no ships remaining to go and collect the oranges; and that instead we'd learned to make marmalade from quince, which was home-grown.

'Ah,' said Whimbrel, 'I see.'

He was still holding his notepad in his hand, and when I looked at it I saw that he had written only one word: LONGITUDE?

10

Of course, the life of an officer-of-state wasn't all work and no play. One bright afternoon Sanderling and I walked across to the far side of the park. We'd heard there was a boating lake, and sure enough when we arrived at the water's edge we saw a short jetty with a dozen vessels tied alongside. They were attractive little rowing boats, each with their oars shipped, and all painted different colours. At the end of the jetty was a green hut in which a man was sitting. When he saw us he walked over and joined us on the shore.

'Afternoon, sir,' he said to each of us in turn.

'Afternoon,' we both replied.

'What can I do for you gentlemen?'

'We thought we might like to hire a boat,' said Sanderling.

'Oh, yes?'

'It looks a bit quiet at the moment.'

'Well, it is rather late in the season, sir.'

'So I expect you'll welcome a little extra business?'

'That depends, sir.'

I was beginning to develop an unwelcome feeling about this character; or more particularly about his way of addressing us as 'sir'. His attitude was different again to that of Greylag, Hobby or Gallinule. The manner in which he said 'sir' was almost insolent, as though he was quite used to calling people 'sir' if they deserved it; but in our case he was reserving judgement.

'How much does it cost?' enquired Sanderling.

'It's a penny a go, sir,' said the boatman.

Sanderling then reached into his pocket and produced his stipendiary sixpence.

'That should cover it,' he said.

'I'm afraid it doesn't, sir,' replied the boatman.

'Why not?'

'I require half-a-crown deposit, sir, to insure against accidental loss or damage.'

'How can we possibly lose a boat on this lake,' demanded Sanderling, 'when we can clearly see across to the other side?'

'You might sink, sir,' came the reply.

'We haven't got half-a-crown,' I said flatly. 'We've got a shilling between us.'

'I'm sorry,' said the boatman, 'but it can't be helped.'

All of a sudden Sanderling took hold of my sleeve and drew me aside to confer.

'You keep him talking,' he said. 'I'll be back as quickly as I can.'

He stalked away and was soon lost from sight amongst the trees. Meanwhile I engaged the boatman in small talk. We discussed the weather, which we agreed was clement for the time of year and therefore liable to change any day soon. In fact, he suspected that more rain was very close by. Then we discussed the excellent condition of the rowing boats, and he told me that he painted them all by hand once a year. Each boat had its own combination of colours, which were carefully preserved from one season to the next.

'That's very commendable,' I remarked. 'I'm impressed.'

'It's not a question of anyone being impressed, sir,' said the boatman. 'It's a question of doing something properly if it's going to be done at all.'

A minute later Sanderling returned. His appearance had changed somewhat because he now had an unusual black hat on his head. It was worn 'fore and aft' and curled downwards at each end. Displayed on the front was the imperial crest.

Sanderling marched directly on to the jetty and stepped into the first boat he came to. As he did so it rocked slightly, but he managed to keep his feet.

'In the name of the admiralty I am commandeering this vessel,' he announced.

To my surprise the boatman snapped to attention. 'Aye aye, sir,' he said, 'aye aye.'

He then began fussing around the boat, making sure everything was 'shipshape', as he put it. He examined the oars to check they were secure in the rowlocks; he coiled the mooring rope; and he sponged the bilges for good measure.

'There you are, sir,' he said. 'Take her out for as long as you wish.'

I joined Sanderling in the boat and we pushed off from the jetty. Once we'd drifted out of earshot I asked him how he knew his ploy would work.

'Former naval man,' Sanderling explained. 'They actually like taking orders but you have to approach them in the correct way.'

'How do you know he was in the navy?'

'He has an earring.'

'Oh,' I said, 'I didn't notice.'

So it was that Sanderling and I spent a very pleasant afternoon rowing up and down the lake. At the periphery was a reedbed, so we poked around in there for a while and scared up a few ducks. Then we realised that another figure had appeared on the jetty: a man in a crimson coat.

'It's the Player King,' said Sanderling. 'I met him earlier.'

'Yes,' I said, 'I've met him too.'

We watched as Gallinule spoke briefly with the boatman. Next moment he was helped into a boat and set off rowing across the lake.

'Why didn't he have to jump through hoops like we did?' I asked.

Sanderling offered no answer.

On an empty lake it was quite natural for the only two boats to gravitate towards one another, which they duly did.

'Ahoy there!' called Gallinule as he drew near.

Sanderling was still wearing his admiral's hat, but he refrained from a maritime greeting. He merely said hello in reply.

'How are you, Gallinule?' I asked. 'I haven't seen you for a day or two.'

'We've been very busy,' Gallinule replied. 'We had to pay a visit to the counting house.'

'Really?'

'Needed to arrange a loan,' he added, 'just to tide us over, you understand.'

'Any luck?'

'Oh yes,' said Gallinule, 'the Chancellor was most accommodating.'

He then went on to tell Sanderling and me that we really must call in at the Maypole when we had the chance.

'We had a marvellous time last night,' he said. 'The beer was flowing freely; there was music playing; and there were lots of dancing girls.'

When he heard this piece of news Sanderling said nothing, and after a while we rowed away. He had still said nothing when we reached the jetty and handed the boat in.

'Never mind,' I said, 'it can't be helped.'

'No,' he replied, 'it never can be helped, can it?'

The hour was approaching five o'clock and the sun was beginning to set over the royal palace. I thought Sanderling looked quite crestfallen in his admiral's hat as we went our separate ways.

'I'm going over to see Whimbrel this evening,' I said. 'Why don't you come along too?'

'No thanks,' he said, 'I think I'll stay in and learn to tie some nautical knots.'

In the event it was probably fortunate that Sanderling didn't come to the observatory. When I arrived I found Whimbrel waiting for a very special guest.

'The Player King has requested a guided tour,' he said. 'He'll be here soon.'

Whimbrel was becoming more of an expert on the stars as time went by. He could now recognise several constellations without reference to his charts; and he was getting to grips with the movements of the planets. Furthermore, he had been back to the library and found out the meaning of longitude.

'It actually has nothing to do with astronomy,' he declared.

'Hasn't it?' I asked.

'Latitude, yes,' he said, 'longitude, no.'

I absorbed this information with a furrowed brow. Meanwhile, Whimbrel went to a window and looked out.

'Excellent,' he concluded. 'A fine, clear sky.'

Nonetheless, I sensed that Whimbrel was rather edgy, as if he wasn't particularly looking forward to the guided tour. He hesitated for a moment before turning away from the window.

'Listen,' he said, 'there's something I've been meaning to ask your opinion about.'

'What sort of something?' I enquired.

'Well, it's this Player King,' he said, 'this Gallinule.'

'What about him?'

'Don't you think he acts as if he owns the place?'

'He acts as if he acts,' I replied. 'That's for certain.'

'Seriously though,' Whimbrel continued, 'haven't you noticed how he makes himself at home everywhere he goes;

and how closed doors simply open at his every whim and fancy? He practically invited himself on this guided tour and I could hardly say no, could I?'

'Suppose not,' I said. 'So what are you driving at exactly?'

'It's just that there's this tradition about the emperor going around in disguise to gauge the true lie of the land.'

'And you think this could be him?'

'I don't know,' said Whimbrel. 'For a while Brambling and I thought it was you.'

'Me?' I exclaimed, astounded. 'How can I be the emperor in disguise?'

'Well, we didn't think it was any of the others.'

'So you presumed it must be me?'

'Yes.'

'I can assure you it isn't.'

'Then along came Gallinule.'

'A much more likely contender.'

'Agreed.'

'But surely he's just an actor?'

'So why has nobody laid eyes on the other seven players he's supposed to be with?'

'Good question.'

'He visited the counting house this afternoon and poor Brambling felt he had no choice but to lend him half-a-crown.'

'But that's equivalent to five sixpences!'

'Precisely,' said Whimbrel. 'He obviously has a high opinion of his own worth; and he talks constantly in the royal "we".'

'As if to the manner born?'

'It's quite possible.'

'Hmm,' I said thoughtfully. ' "Find the Emperor": sounds like a parlour game.'

Just then we heard a voice rising from the doorway down below. It had a clear, resonant tone that carried easily to our ears.

'Anybody home?'

'Hello!' Whimbrel called back. 'Yes, please come up.'

The iron staircase clanged as Gallinule made his entrance.

'Absolutely marvellous piece of architecture!' he said, by way of greeting. 'So this is the world-famous royal observatory of Fallowfields!'

Whimbrel appeared slightly taken aback, as if he had never considered the place in such august terms before. I thought about the cake and realised that it, too, was 'world-famous'.

Gallinule turned out to be the perfect guest. Before the guided tour he presented Whimbrel with a bagful of lions and tigers from the confectioner's shop.

'Hobby has a wonderful selection of sweets,' Gallinule told us. 'We hardly knew which to choose.'

During the course of the tour he asked sensible questions that Whimbrel was able to answer in an informative way. He was especially keen to find out where north was, and seemed impressed when Whimbrel showed him the 'easy' method for locating it. Finally we went up on to the roof for an overall view of the sky.

'I'm sorry I can't let you have a look through the telescope,' said Whimbrel, 'but I'm afraid it's jammed.'

'Oh, you should have mentioned it before,' said Gallinule. 'We could have brought Mestolone with us.'

'Who's Mestolone?'

'He's one of our strolling players. He specialises in all the minor roles. You know: captains, soldiers, messengers, attendants, porters, murderers. You name it: he plays it.'

'What's all that got to do with my telescope?' Whimbrel enquired.

'Mestolone is also a gifted handyman,' Gallinule explained. 'He builds all our scenery and he can mend anything. We'll send him over tomorrow afternoon.'

'Oh, right, thanks,' said Whimbrel. 'So you really are an actor then?'

'Of course,' Gallinule replied. 'Actor par excellence!'

11

At ten o'clock on Monday morning, Smew called the register.

'Chancellor?'

'Present.'

'Postmaster?'

'Present.'

'Astronomer?'

'Present.'

'Comptroller?'

'Present.'

'Surveyor?'

'Present.'

'Pellitory?'

'Present.'

'Composer?'

'Present.'

'His Exalted Highness, the Majestic Emperor of the Realms, Dominions, Colonies and Commonwealth of Greater Fallowfields?'

There was no response.

'Absent,' said Smew.

'Oh, that reminds me,' said Wryneck. 'We've received another letter from the emperor.'

From his inside pocket he produced an envelope. It was addressed to the cabinet and bore the imperial seal.

'Before we open it can I have a look at the postmark?' said Garganey.

'Certainly,' said Wryneck.

It transpired that the letter had been posted locally on the previous evening.

'I'm quite pleased about that,' Garganey remarked. 'Perhaps my measures are taking effect at last.'

He opened the envelope to reveal an imperial edict:

BY ORDER OF HIS MAJESTY

THE EMPEROR OF GREATER FALLOWFIELDS

IT IS COMMANDED THAT

FROM HENCEFORTH THE SUN WILL SET DAILY AT

FIVE O'CLOCK.

The edict was passed around the table so that each officer-of-state could see it for himself.

'Direct and to the point,' remarked Dotterel.

We all agreed about that.

Privately, I considered this latest demand to be simply outrageous. It was one thing to restrict the sale of sweets or beer for reasons of public morality; it was quite another to dictate the hour when the sun set. Exactly who, I wondered, did the emperor think he was?

Still, there was no point in voicing my reservations to the others. An edict was an edict and had to be obeyed. I was only glad that it wasn't my job to enact it.

'Well, now, Whimbrel,' said Smew. 'This looks like your department.'

'Yes,' Whimbrel replied, 'I thought it might be.'

The edict had finished its journey around the table and now lay in Whimbrel's hands. He stared at it blankly for several long moments before rising to his feet.

'If you'll excuse me, gentlemen,' he said, 'I'd like to take this back to the observatory so that I can study its implications in depth.'

'And then you'll report back, will you?' enquired Smew.

'Yes,' said Whimbrel, 'although I might be some time.'

Having devolved such a heavy responsibility on to Whimbrel, the rest of us resumed work on our play. It was a fractious rehearsal to say the least. For a start, I was enrolled to play the ghost in Whimbrel's absence. I spent a good deal of time going in and out of the room, and sitting down in other people's places. At one point I accidentally chose the emperor's empty chair and earned a stern rebuke from Wryneck. Nor were matters helped by Smew's repeated assertion that the king was the only person who couldn't see the ghost, which I was now beginning to doubt. Then Dotterel mentioned that we kept referring to Garganey as the king when he was in fact a usurper. Furthermore,

Dotterel said that he had found at least three other kings in the text.

'This should help clarify the situation,' he announced. He had with him a wooden box which he now opened. Inside was a golden crown. He placed it on the table and Wryneck immediately took it up in both hands.

'Where did you find this?' he asked.

Wryneck uttered these words as though he was collating evidence for some unnamed future inquisition. His voice was flat and toneless, but the question was nevertheless insistent.

'I was conducting an inventory of the imperial artefacts,' said Dotterel. 'It was in the royal workshop being smartened up for the coronation.'

'So it's the emperor's crown?' said Sanderling.

'Sort of,' said Dotterel. 'Actually this is the spare crown: the lightweight model used in public ceremonies and processions.'

He removed the crown from Wryneck's grasp and tossed it across the table towards Sanderling.

'Here,' he said, 'catch!'

To everyone's surprise Garganey intercepted it in mid-air and put it on his head.

'You can't do that,' said Wryneck. There was a sudden note of disquiet in his voice.

'I've done it,' replied Garganey. 'I presume you intended this as a stage prop, Dotterel?'

'A temporary stage prop, yes,' Dotterel answered. 'For rehearsal purposes only, you understand.'

'Just to remind everybody who's king and who isn't?'

'Indeed.'

'And where's the proper crown?' I enquired.

'I've no idea,' said Dotterel. 'It's reputed to be made from solid gold, whereas the spare one is base metal and gold paint.'

'Base metal or no base metal,' said Garganey, 'this crown bears the imperial writ.'

He was still wearing it on his head, a fact that appeared to be causing Wryneck considerable unease. Smew, meanwhile, had fallen unusually silent. Finally, Garganey lifted the crown off his head and placed it back on the table.

Just then the door opened and Whimbrel came in. He nodded at everyone before taking his usual seat next to mine. Somehow he seemed very self-assured; he even looked larger in stature than when he went out.

'How did you get on?' I asked.

'Very successfully,' he replied. 'I think I've found the solution.'

'Which is?'

'Well,' said Whimbrel, 'plainly we can't alter the sunset; therefore, we'll have to alter the clocks.'

A stir went around the room.

'Good idea,' I remarked. 'I never thought of that.'

'I've consulted my tables,' Whimbrel continued, 'and it so happens that the sun set yesterday evening at exactly five o'clock. According to my calculations we need to put the clocks forward by two minutes every day.'

'To guarantee a sunset at five?' said Smew.

'Correct,' said Whimbrel. 'Now, Dotterel, I remember you once told me you were in charge of all the artisans.'

'Yes,' said Dotterel, 'I am.'

'So presumably you're in charge of all the clocks as well?'

'Yes.'

'Then it looks as if you're going to be very busy.'

As the gravity of the disclosure dawned on Dotterel he visibly turned pale. There were dozens of public clocks in the royal quarter, let alone the thousands situated all across the empire. For the edict to be carried out effectively, every one of these clocks would have to be altered daily. Whimbrel's work was done: Dotterel's, apparently, was only just beginning.

'I must set things in train at once,' he said, heading for the door.

'What about this?' said Smew, indicating the ceremonial crown. 'Shall I keep it safe in the library?'

'Yes, please,' said Dotterel. 'That would be a great help.' He was about to leave when he paused at the door and turned to Garganey. 'I'll need to confer with you about informing all the clock-keepers. They'll require a letter of instruction.'

'The postmen aren't going to like it,' declared Garganey. 'They'll have to get up two minutes earlier every day.'

'That can't be helped,' said Wryneck.

'I know it can't be helped,' said Garganey, 'but they're still not going to like it.'

During all this flurry Whimbrel sat motionless at the table. I thought he looked quite pleased with himself.

'Don't forget you've got a visitor this afternoon,' I reminded him.

'Oh, yes, the handyman,' said Whimbrel. 'I almost forgot.'

Being no longer required in the cabinet room, we made our excuses and left. A short while later we arrived at the observatory to find a man waiting outside the door.

'Mestolone, I presume?' said Whimbrel.

The man was completely unlike Gallinule. His coat was black and he spoke plainly.

'You've got a defective telescope, I understand?'

'Yes,' said Whimbrel, 'would you like to come up?'

The three of us clanged our way to the top of the building. It was another bright autumn afternoon and the telescope glinted in the sunlight. Mestolone placed his hand on the barrel and gave it a gentle nudge. As usual it failed to move. Then he walked around and examined it from the other side.

'Aha,' he said. 'Have you got a sixpence by any chance?'

'Of course,' said Whimbrel. He reached into his pocket, produced his stipendiary sixpence and handed it over.

Next moment there was a *clunk*. Then Mestolone swung the telescope upwards and peered through the eyepiece.

'There you are,' he said. 'It works now.'

'Marvellous,' said Whimbrel.

It took him a little while to get used to directing and focusing the device correctly, but soon he was happily gazing across the park at various buildings.

In the meantime I stepped around to Mestolone's side of

the telescope. He showed me the slot where he'd dropped the sixpence in.

'So it wasn't broken?'

'No.'

Another *clunk* signalled that Whimbrel's time was up.

'Let's have a go,' I said, fumbling for my own sixpence. I looked first at the cake, focusing on the main door and imagining Greylag and the orchestra busily at work inside. I hadn't dropped in on them for several days now. I wondered casually how the overture was progressing, and whether it was nearing fruition. Then I turned the telescope the other way and tried to see in through the windows of the royal palace. I thought that maybe I could even catch a glimpse of our reclusive emperor! Another *clunk*, however, put paid to that idea.

'You don't get very long, do you?' remarked Whimbrel.

'Well,' I said, 'at least you've now got something to spend your sixpence on.'

Nonetheless, we agreed that we'd both wasted our money on this occasion.

'We should have looked across at those plumes of smoke,' said Whimbrel. 'I forgot all about them in the excitement.'

We turned to the east and, sure enough, a plume of smoke was rising. It seemed to be a good deal closer than the last time I'd been up here; furthermore, the vague line in the terrain was less ill-defined than before.

'What do you think that smoke is?' I asked Mestolone. 'We think there must be some foresters working over there.'

Mestolone looked doubtful.

'Foresters usually work in squares and oblongs,' he said. 'These people appear to be coming in a straight line.'

Mestolone continued staring in the same direction for quite a while but he offered no suggestion about the plume of smoke. He was a quiet man but now he had become even quieter. It struck me that he was maybe feeling a little homesick. After all, he and the other players had travelled a long way to get here.

Whimbrel thanked Mestolone for his help and invited him to stay for tea. Then we took a last look eastward before descending the iron ladder. The telescope would have to wait until Whimbrel and I had received our replacement sixpences.

'Where do you all come from, Mestolone?' I asked, while Whimbrel was boiling the kettle.

'Down in the south-east,' said Mestolone. 'Our country was a fledgling democracy.'

'Was?' I said.

'I'm afraid so,' replied Mestolone. 'Our king was in exile and we were being ruled by a parliament.'

Now he looked very sad indeed and I began to wish I hadn't started the conversation. Still, it was too late now.

'I thought parliaments were supposed to be a good thing,' I ventured.

'They are,' affirmed Mestolone, 'but our parliament tried much too hard. They spent hours and hours debating every subject under the sun; and then they made laws which they couldn't enforce.'

'Such as?'

'Well,' said Mestolone, 'take the Act of Emparkment, for example. This stipulated that no man could graze more than one hundredth part of any common land.'

'Sounds fair enough to me,' I said.

'That was the trouble,' said Mestolone. 'The Act was drawn up in the name of fairness but without considering the consequences. Common land couldn't be fenced off, which meant that grazing animals were able to stray out of their allotted "hundreds". Hence, the graziers broke the law without doing anything wrong. The whole Act was thrown into question; and there were many others in a similar vein. It was all most unsatisfactory.'

'What happened then?'

'There was uproar in the House,' said Mestolone, 'and one night the Speaker's Chair was stolen. This gave certain elements an excuse to demand the dissolution of parliament. Not long afterwards our country was offered the usual protection; an offer duly accepted by the same elements. That was when we decided to leave.'

'So you're migrants rather than travellers?'

'I'm afraid so,' said Mestolone.

I had to admit that he'd lost me slightly when he referred to 'certain elements' and 'the usual protection'. Presumably he thought I knew what he was talking about, but actually I didn't. I could tell by Whimbrel's face that he didn't either. All we could do was provide tea and sympathy.

Thankfully, Mestolone wasn't the kind of person to dwell on his misfortunes. As soon as he'd had his tea he announced that he must be going because Gallinule was beginning rehearsals that very day.

'What are you rehearsing?' I asked.

'It's a play about ambition, treason and murder,' said Mestolone.

12

The recent imperial edict was going to take a lot of getting used to. The first thing everybody had to do in the morning was put their clocks and watches forward by two minutes; this meant they had to get up a little earlier than the day before. Soon people would be waking up in darkness. The postmen, of course, were already accustomed to rising early. All the same they didn't take kindly to the new regime, just as Garganey had predicted. It wasn't long before some letters began going astray for days on end, while others got lost in the post entirely. Garganey held talks with the postmen's representatives but to no avail, and eventually he was forced to abandon his so-called efficiency measures. Accordingly, the postmen resumed their practice of having breakfast half-way through the morning. Even so, they still weren't happy about the edict. They began to call it 'the conspiracy of the clocks'.

'Perhaps you should give them a pay rise,' proposed Whimbrel.

'I can't do that,' said Garganey. 'Their wages are fixed by imperial decree.'

'Does a decree carry the same weight as an edict?' I asked.

'Apparently, yes,' said Garganey.

Whimbrel and I were on our way to see Brambling. We needed to replace our stipendiary sixpences.

'Why don't you come along too?' I suggested. 'Who knows what's hidden in the coffers.'

We arrived at the counting house and found Brambling perusing his ledger. It was lying open at the page that dealt with stipends.

'This is all highly irregular,' he said, when we submitted our claims. 'It says nothing here about a telescope.'

'But I need it for my work as Astronomer Royal,' objected Whimbrel.

'Well, you've managed all right without it up to now,' replied Brambling. 'Why do you need a telescope all of a sudden?'

In this light, my own claim for a new sixpence was even more groundless. After all, I had no need for a telescope to carry out my 'work' as Principal Composer. On the other hand, I was entitled to my stipend by imperial statute, and Brambling knew this. As Whimbrel and I sat facing him across his desk, I became convinced that he was simply toying with us because he held the purse strings. Finally, after much prevarication, he relented. He opened the drawer of his desk, took out the tin money box and unlocked it.

'Ah,' he said. 'Empty.'

He then went over to the iron-bound treasure chest in the corner of the room. This too was locked, and only after a further delay was the key found and the lid raised. Inside, it was full to the brim with sixpences, shillings and half-crowns. Whimbrel, Garganey and I joined Brambling in the corner and we all stood gazing down at the gleaming hoard.

'No wonder there's hardly any money in circulation,' I said. 'It's all in here.'

'This isn't for circulation,' replied Brambling. 'This is the reserve currency.'

'What's it reserved for?'

'A rainy day.'

'But it rains half the year in Fallowfields!'

'It can't be helped,' said Brambling.

He selected a sixpence each for me and Whimbrel, and then prepared to close the lid again.

'This is preposterous,' said Garganey suddenly. 'My postmen are struggling to get by on a penny a day, and meanwhile there's all this money lying unused!'

'I wouldn't say they were struggling,' said Brambling. 'They're in the public houses every night.'

'It's not up to you to decide how they spend their earnings,' retorted Garganey.

'No,' said Brambling, 'but this treasure chest is my responsibility.'

'It seems very unfair to me,' remarked Whimbrel.

'Unfairness is what keeps the world going round,' announced Brambling. 'These coins are staying firmly under lock and key.'

Brambling's approach to money had certainly changed during the course of his tenure. Anybody would have thought that it was his own funds he was paying out, rather than the imperial coinage.

'No more sixpences for sightseeing,' he proclaimed, as the three of us departed.

'Damned cheek,' muttered Garganey. He was still clearly enraged.

'It's good to see you have such deep concerns for your workforce,' observed Whimbrel. 'After all, they can be quite troublesome at times.'

'Oh, they're troublesome without a doubt,' said Garganey. 'Nevertheless, I cannot simply abandon them to their fate. As Postmaster General I have obligations not only to the empire but also towards those who are dependent on me. I've come to realise that only by commanding their loyalty will I ever make the postmen more efficient.'

Garganey's words were still ringing in my ears as I neared the park and headed for the cake. It struck me that maybe I should try to do more for my serfs. True enough, the postmen received a penny a day for their labours and were therefore less deserving of sympathy. All the same, Garganey did his best to provide for them. When I thought of Greylag and his unpaid musicians in their threadbare coats I couldn't help feeling a pang of guilt.

I was still pondering all this when I entered the cake through the main doorway and looked down towards the orchestra. They had evidently just finished playing. I could tell this from the way they were attending to their instruments and talking quietly amongst themselves. Meanwhile, Greylag was standing on the podium making small changes to his manuscript. All appeared to be normal, and I was about to proceed down the aisle when I noticed Wryneck sitting in one of the hard seats at the rear of the auditorium. This was the second time he'd turned up uninvited. Presumably he'd been snooping on the orchestra again and I decided to say something to that effect. When he saw me approaching, however, he waved his hand in acknowledgement.

'This overture,' he said, before I had a chance to speak. 'Did you specify a particular duration?'

'Not really,' I replied, 'though I expect it'll be in the order of fifteen minutes or so.'

'I see.'

'Why do you ask?'

'I've just sat through it from beginning to end,' said Wryneck, 'and it ran to almost an hour.'

'Well, if you didn't like it,' I snapped, 'why bother staying so long?'

My raised voice must have caught the ear of some of the musicians, because they began to peer in our direction.

'I didn't say I didn't like it,' said Wryneck. 'As a matter of fact I believe you have a work of genius on your hands.'

'Really?'

'Moreover, the orchestra seems to be in peak form,' he continued. 'I'm most impressed by the quality of their attack and decay.'

'They practise day and night,' I pointed out.

Wryneck nodded his approval.

'This overture is an exceptional piece of music,' he said, 'and I was simply going to suggest that you should maybe consider it as a stand–alone composition, rather than a mere prelude to a play.'

'Oh,' I said, 'yes, I'll certainly bear your comments in mind.'

'Thank you,' rejoined Wryneck, 'and congratulations.'

He rose from his seat and together we walked down to the orchestra pit. The musicians had fallen silent at the sight of Wryneck. Greylag was now occupying his former seat amongst the violins. I acknowledged him vaguely as we passed.

'I hope you don't mind my asking,' said Wryneck, 'but would it be possible for me to take a turn on the piano for a few minutes?'

'Of course,' I replied. 'I didn't know you played.'

'I'm a little rusty,' he said, 'but I had lessons as a child.'

'Help yourself,' I said, indicating the piano.

He sat down and started playing without a score. I recognised the piece at once: a well-known sonata that spoke gently of romance and lost love. Wryneck was plainly an accomplished pianist. As he continued his rendition he seemed to be completely absorbed in the music, to the point of being visibly moved by it, and I realised I had made a classic mistake. I'd assumed that because Wryneck carried out his duties to the letter he somehow lacked any feelings or even personality. This was a common error in public life: people who did their jobs properly were generally thought to be heartless and uncaring. Wryneck was a prime example of such a fallacy: on the face of it he was an ambitious and unscrupulous servant of the state, bent only on executing a stream of imperial edicts, yet here he was playing the piano beautifully, as though his whole existence depended on it. Behind his official role as Pellitory-of-the-Wall he was obviously an ordinary person with ordinary desires. Clearly I had misjudged him.

Eventually, Wryneck ceased playing and turned to me.

'This piano', he said, 'has seen better days.'

Just then a distant clock struck a quarter to three. Or more correctly, the clock struck a quarter to three in 'adjusted time' as it was now generally known.

Wryneck glanced at his watch. 'Are you coming along to Smew's talk?'

'Has a fortnight passed already?' I asked.

Indeed it had, which meant we needed to set off immediately towards the library if we wished to arrive before the talk began. Wryneck was known for his punctuality, so I knew that all I had to do was keep in step in order to avoid being late. As it was we entered the reading room with a couple of minutes to spare. None of the other officers-of-state had turned up; nor was there any sign of Gallinule, despite his fulsome bout of enthusiasm at the previous talk. For my part I was in the perfect frame of mind for some scholarly improvement, having being buoyed up by Wryneck's praise of the new overture. It was only as I settled into my seat that it occurred to me I'd neglected to speak to Greylag.

At exactly three o'clock (adjusted time), Smew began his talk. Ostensibly the subject was the history of the empire, but today he had chosen to approach it from an oblique angle.

'So here we had an empire,' he began, 'that considered herself to be at the centre of the civilised world; whose success depended on the willingness of other states to revolve around her, to emulate her, and to bow to her supposed superiority.'

Smew paused.

'Or was this apparent success founded on a grand conceit?' he asked. 'Could it be possible that our neighbours actually took little interest in what we got up to; that they were merely playing us along to keep us quiet?'

I wasn't sure to which 'neighbours' Smew was alluding here. As far as I'd gathered from his earlier talks, the realms, dominions, colonies and commonwealth were all fully acquiescent to the empire's benign guidance. Yet now he seemed to be implying the opposite. For a moment I wondered if I hadn't been paying attention properly. To my left I noticed Wryneck making his usual copious notes, a fact that suggested I'd missed something.

'I'm talking about the so-called "friendly" cities in the east,' said Smew, 'although "friendly" is probably a misnomer: they've never been particularly "friendly" to each other or anyone else for that matter. They earned the name "friendly" as expressed in the term "friendly rivalry" rather than "friendly co-operation". They were never in league with one another and remained rigorously independent. Unaffected by external spheres of influence, they were completely beyond the gravitational pull of the empire. Instead, each city followed a linear course that took it hurtling headlong towards its own destiny. They differed from us in many ways. For instance, we acquired gold by exploiting our sovereignty at sea, whereas they mined it directly out of the ground; our clocks had pendulums, while theirs employed a spring-balance mechanism; we favoured amateurs: they used professionals; we had palaces: they had castles; and so on. Our mastery of the seaways gave us command of the coast. Consequently, their people were confined many miles inland. In due course they became expert civil engineers: as well as constructing mines, they dug canals, drained the marshes, built bridges and finally developed iron railways. Our prowess at sailing meant we had no need for such innovations. We proudly carried on with our seafaring traditions, and hardly took any notice as these cities took turns to rise and fall.'

Smew paused again, and it appeared as though the talk had come to a natural conclusion, 'rise and fall' being a suitably ringing phrase with which to close. I was surprised, then, when he continued speaking:

'We did not allow these cities to become entirely isolated, however. The empire's sole concession to the east was to send her sons to one or other of their great universities. We recognised that in their struggle for improvement they had cultivated some important seats of learning. Hence, each prospective emperor enrolled at a revered institution whilst still an uncrowned princeling. The theory was that he'd study and learn thoroughly the ways of the east; then after a certain period he would return home and, following much thought and introspection, reject them. It was a tried and tested thesis, effectively put to use by generations of emperors right up to this very day.'

Now Wryneck closed his notepad and put away his pen, which told me for sure that the talk was over.

'I never knew that,' I said, 'about the emperor going away to university.'

Smew said nothing in reply, but instead stood silently gazing at me from behind his lectern. Again I wondered if there was some important point that Wryneck had grasped but I clearly hadn't. Or perhaps Smew was allowing a few more moments for it to sink in. Either way, I rose from my seat feeling somewhat bemused.

'Like some tea?' said Smew.

I'd decided in advance to say no if such an invitation was made, because I really ought to get back and attend to the needs of the orchestra.

'Yes, thank you,' I said. 'That would be nice.'

'Lemon curd and toasted soldiers?'

'Even better.'

Smew pulled the tasselled cord to alert Shrike. Meanwhile, Wryneck and I settled down in the comfortable chairs by the bay window. When Smew joined us he chose the chair nearest to his desk, on top of which lay Dotterel's box containing the ceremonial crown.

'Shouldn't that be locked away somewhere safe?' I enquired.

'It's safe enough here in the library,' replied Smew. 'Either Wryneck or myself are always present.'

A few minutes later Shrike returned with a fully laden tray. As he handed us our portions of toast the clock struck five and the setting sun cast its warm rays through the window.

'Just perfect for teatime,' I remarked.

'Yes,' said Smew. 'Marmalade for breakfast; lemon curd for tea.'

13

Whimbrel could always be found at the observatory, studying his charts and tables and peering at the sky through his telescope. He seemed to do nothing else these days. The only place he ever went was down to the counting house for his replacement sixpence. Brambling had finally accepted that Whimbrel needed to use his telescope constantly, and now always kept an appropriate coin ready at hand.

'It's a pity you don't get more than a few minutes,' said Whimbrel, after yet another *clunk* had signalled the end of his time.

'What are you looking at tonight?' I asked.

'The Pole Star,' he replied. 'Did you know that if you gaze at it long enough the whole sky appears to revolve around it?'

The thought occurred to me that Whimbrel really ought to get out more, and I told him as much.

'There's nowhere to go, though, is there?' he said.

'Not usually, no,' I conceded, 'but tomorrow evening sees the first public showcase for my overture. Come along to the cake and have a listen.'

Recently I had redoubled my efforts to spend more time with Greylag and the orchestra. I'd sat in on a run-through and together we'd decided that no further improvements could be made to the work. Smew's play was still nowhere near completion, so I'd decided to take Wryneck's advice and present the overture as a 'stand-alone' composition.

'Very well done, Greylag,' I said, after the final rehearsal. 'Now we'll put it to the test of a proper audience.'

By a 'proper audience' I meant only the officers-of-state, of course, as it was pointless expecting the emperor to turn up. I spent the next morning going around to the various departments informing everybody about the forthcoming performance. Most people accepted the invitation willingly, but Dotterel demurred.

'I just don't have the time to spare,' he said. 'I'm striving perpetually to make sure all the clocks are correct.'

'Don't your artisans take care of that?' I enquired.

'They're doing their best,' said Dotterel, 'but to tell the truth we're only just managing to keep on top of it all.'

True enough, Dotterel looked worn out. His eyes were leaden and he seemed to be on the verge of nodding off as he worked through his checklist of clocks.

'Between you and me,' he said, 'this latest demand of the emperor is simply absurd. It's one thing for him to miss a few cabinet meetings; it's quite another to turn the whole empire upside down just so that he can enjoy the sunset from his palace window.'

'Do you think that's the reason then?'

'I can't see any other explanation,' said Dotterel, 'unless His Majesty is deliberately trying to exhaust all his subjects.'

'That's hardly likely.'

'To be frank,' continued Dotterel, 'there's far too much power concentrated in one pair of hands and it can only lead to disaster. It reminds me of that legend about a king who believes the tide will turn at his mere command. His courtiers are doubtful, so he orders them to set his throne upon the seashore. Then, when the tide fails to turn, his weakness is exposed.'

'No,' I said, 'you're wrong there.'

'What do you mean wrong?' snapped Dotterel. 'It's a well-known legend!'

'I'm fully aware of that,' I said, 'but it's the courtiers who think the king can turn the tide, not the other way round. He shows them he can't to demonstrate the limits of his power.'

'Oh,' said Dotterel, 'I see.'

'You can look it up in the library.'

'I'd like to,' he said, 'but I don't have the time.'

'Talking of the library,' I said, 'you know you left Smew in charge of the ceremonial crown?'

'Yes.'

'Well, when you found it you mentioned it was being smartened up for the coronation.'

'That's right,' said Dotterel. 'I hope Smew's looking after it properly.'

'It's perfectly safe,' I affirmed.

'Good.'

'Going back to this matter of the coronation, though. When's it going to happen, exactly?'

'As soon as the emperor's ready, I suppose.'

'So he's never been crowned?'

'Not as far as I know.'

Dotterel gave me a tired look, and I realised that he was beginning to wilt under all my questioning.

'My apologies, Dotterel,' I said, 'I'll leave you in peace now. So you definitely won't be attending tonight?'

'I'm afraid not,' he said. 'Sorry.'

My next port of call was the observatory. Whimbrel had already agreed to come to the performance, but I knew that he would need reminding again. The door was open so I made my way up the iron spiral, expecting to find him hard at work over his chart table. When I reached the top there was no sign of him, though, which meant he must be on the roof.

'Is that you?' he called down, when he heard me ascending the ladder.

'Yes,' I said. 'What are you up to?'

'I'm using the telescope.'

'Isn't that a waste of sixpence?'

'Why?'

'Because it's broad daylight!' I said. 'It's ten o'clock in the morning!'

'Come and see for yourself.'

I emerged through the tiny door and discovered Whimbrel pointing the telescope not at the sky, but due east. A loud *clunk*, however, told me that his time had just expired.

'Blast,' he said.

I looked to the east. Some miles away a plume of smoke was rising from amongst the trees; beyond it a straight, dark line cut through the terrain and extended all the way back to the horizon.

'Good grief,' I said. 'It's getting nearer.'

'Have you got your sixpence on you?' Whimbrel enquired.

I didn't really want to use up my stipend, but Whimbrel's tone was most insistent so I handed it over. He dropped the coin in the slot and peered through the eyepiece.

'Appears to be quite a lot of activity going on over there,' he said. 'I can see some tents and several piles of felled timber. Those foresters are certainly busy.'

'I don't think they are foresters,' I said.

'How do you mean?' said Whimbrel.

He continued to hog the telescope.

'Let's have a look and I'll tell you.'

Reluctantly, he moved out of the way and I took his place. I was a few seconds getting used to the telescope, but eventually I focused on the apparent source of the smoke. It was some kind of funnel. Then I heard a *clunk*.

'Blast,' I said.

'What do you think it is?' asked Whimbrel.

'I don't know,' I replied, 'but I'm sure it's not foresters.'

Having no further sixpences we resumed our vigil without the aid of the telescope; but we saw little apart from the lingering plume of smoke. We remained on the roof for another quarter of an hour. Then, from somewhere in the distance, there came a shrill piping sound. A minute passed and we heard it again, only fainter this time; and now the plume of smoke seemed to be moving away.

'I've been watching for a week,' said Whimbrel. 'It always comes back after a while.'

We descended the iron ladder.

'Look, Whimbrel,' I said, 'I'd prefer if you didn't mention this to any of the others until after tonight's performance. I really don't want any distractions.'

'Oh, yes, tonight's performance,' said Whimbrel. 'It's a good job you reminded me.'

That afternoon I dropped in at the cake to make sure everything was taken care of. I found Greylag and the rest of the orchestra brushing down their frock coats and polishing their boots.

'How are you feeling, Greylag?' I enquired.

'My feelings are unimportant, sir,' he replied. 'It's the music that counts.'

'Of course,' I said. 'We have some important guests tonight so I hope for all our sakes that it goes well.'

'I'm sure it will, sir. It contains all the elements you mentioned.'

This was indeed the case. During the final run-through I had been overwhelmed by the depth of Greylag's creation. The way he'd used music to conjure up the required sense of foreboding, dubiety and hazard was almost uncanny. It promised a very bright future.

'Is there nothing I can do for you, Greylag?' I asked. 'Nothing at all?'

'Well, sir,' he said, 'it would be very pleasant to go out in the fresh air for a change, instead of being cooped up in here all the time.'

'Fresh air?' I said. 'Yes, I can arrange that, Greylag. Consider it done.'

'Thank you, sir.'

'Meanwhile I have some more guests to inform, so good luck and I'll see you afterwards.'

Having contacted Whimbrel, Brambling, Garganey and Sanderling, as well as allowing for Dotterel's absence, there were only two names left on my list: Wryneck and Smew. I went over to the great library in the late afternoon with plenty of time to spare, as the performance wasn't scheduled until seven thirty.

Unusually, the library doors were closed when I arrived. They weren't locked, however, so I went inside and began browsing around the shelves. This was certainly a well-stocked collection of books and I could see why Smew was so attached to his domain. Even so, I didn't think he was quite the expert on literature that he obviously felt himself to be. His interpretation of the play contained some glaring errors, and I'd begun to wonder about the accuracy of his so-called history of the empire. Entertaining as it was, the facts had yet to be proved. When I reached the far end of the shelves I saw that the door to the reading room was also closed. I knocked and entered without waiting for a reply.

Wryneck and Smew were clearly not expecting visitors. Indeed, they appeared mildly surprised to see me. They were sitting in their comfortable chairs by the large bay window. Between them was a tray of tea and toasted soldiers; also a pot of lemon curd. On Smew's desk lay the ceremonial crown. It had been removed from its box and was gleaming in the late-afternoon sunshine.

'Aha,' I said, by way of greeting, 'the unclaimed crown.'

Neither Wryneck nor Smew replied.

I closed the door behind me.

'What I meant,' I continued, 'was that we're still waiting for the coronation to take place.'

'Yes,' said Wryneck.

Smew said nothing.

'So the crown remains unused for the time being.'

They gazed at me with blank expressions.

'Until the emperor claims it,' I ventured.

I didn't seem to be getting through to them.

The clock struck five and the sun began to set. It was a picture of regal splendour: the entire room was instantly bathed in a sumptuous glow, just the same as the day before; and the day before that; and the day before that as well.

Then the truth dawned.

'There was no edict, was there?' I said.

'No,' Smew answered.

'It was all concocted for your personal enjoyment.'

'Yes.'

'What about the emperor?'

'He's not here.'

'Only this pretend crown?'

'Correct.'

Wryneck and Smew had begun to look very uncomfortable. I glanced around at the cups and saucers, the teapot, the plates and the toasted soldiers. I watched the last rays of sunset creep slowly across the room. Finally I passed judgement.

'Rather selfish, wasn't it?'

14

According to Wryneck and Smew they had no choice in the matter. The young emperor had failed to come home from university at the end of term; neither had he written to declare his intentions. With no official word forthcoming, Wryneck and Smew decided they should try to carry on as though everything was normal. They quietly postponed the coronation and continued to hold weekly cabinet meetings. Meanwhile they held court in private.

'Certain traditions needed to be maintained,' said Smew. 'What better symbol of changelessness than tea at five in a sunlit reading room?'

He rose from his chair and put the crown back in its box.

'How long has all this been going on?' I asked.

'Several months,' replied Smew. 'I only discovered the emperor was absent when he neglected to return his library books.'

'You mean he'd borrowed them?'

'Yes.'

'I thought you said it wasn't a lending library.'

'It's different for the emperor,' Smew pointed out. 'He owns the books.'

'Oh.'

'I'm a mere custodian.'

'If you're a mere custodian,' I said, 'what entitled you to take charge of the affairs of state?'

'Wryneck and I felt it was the best course of action,' said Smew, 'to ensure the continuity of the empire.'

From that point of view I conceded they were probably right. All the same, the pair had taken a number of liberties which needed to be addressed.

'What about the edicts?' I enquired. 'I assume they were forgeries.'

'Yes they were,' said Smew. 'We realised we needed the full weight of authority behind us if we were to succeed.'

'So why didn't Garganey get an edict to help him deal with the postmen? That would have been of great use to him.'

'We thought it was too obvious,' Smew replied.

'Well, neither he nor Dotterel are going to be very pleased when they find out about this,' I said. 'You've made both their lives extremely difficult.'

'Are you going to tell them then?'

'Not yet, no,' I said. 'It all has to be untangled very carefully; otherwise the populace could become restless.'

'I'm glad to hear you have a grasp of the situation,' remarked Wryneck.

There was another motive as well, of course. I didn't want anything to interfere with the evening's concert perform- ance. Time was slipping by, so I handed them their invitations and set off towards the cake. I planned to greet the guests as they arrived. I'd also decided that I should ask Gallinule and his companions along, not least because they promised to brighten up the audience. I called in at the Maypole and learnt that they were not at home.

'They're busy rehearsing their play,' said the publican.

As usual he was standing behind his counter polishing glasses.

'Could you pass them a message?' I enquired.

'Certainly,' he said. 'Is it about the Greylag Overture?'

'Oh,' I said, somewhat surprised by the reference, 'yes.'

'Thought so.'

'You know about that then, do you?'

'Everybody knows about it,' he said. 'The word has spread and no doubt they'll be clamouring at the door.'

This was news to me. I'd always assumed that the kind of orchestral music heard at the cake was confined to court circles only. It now appeared I was misinformed. I glanced around the bar and for the first time realised it was deserted.

'Where is everybody?' I asked.

'Queuing up, I imagine,' replied the publican.

I thanked him and hurried off towards the cake. It was nearly seven o'clock and, sure enough, there was a queue at the door that extended right around the circumference of the building. This queue consisted of postmen, artisans and other commoners. They filed through the door in an orderly manner and took their places in the hard seats at the rear of the auditorium. Next to arrive were the officers-of-state, all wearing their dandy coats, and I was pleased to see that even Dotterel had found time to attend. Naturally the strolling players turned up with only minutes to spare. Gallinule made an entrance dressed in all his crimson finery, and such a fuss ensued as he found his seat that anyone would have thought the audience had come to see him, rather than the imperial orchestra.

I joined Whimbrel, Garganey and Sanderling in the soft seats near the front. Brambling, Dotterel, Wryneck and Smew chose the row behind us. Then I watched with pride as Greylag took to the podium. Although he wore the imperial livery, which showed that he was a serf, he had all the bearing of an established conductor. At precisely seven thirty he primed the waiting orchestra and the music began.

Greylag's overture lived up to all expectations. From the plaintive opening tones of the lone oboe, to the gigantic scrunched chords of the finale, it tirelessly swept the audience along in its wake. In some sections the music threatened to return the whole world to primordial chaos; in others it rose from modest simplicity to expressions of colossal stature. I eagerly awaited Greylag's 'deliberate mistake' involving the discordant entry of the hunting horn. I was not disappointed: the effect on the unsuspecting audience was marked.

Only Garganey seemed to misunderstand, much to my annoyance.

'Damn that horn!' I heard him say. 'He's come in too early.'

I was quite pleased a moment later when Garganey was shushed from behind by Wryneck.

At the end came the applause, and Greylag thoroughly deserved it. One or two of my colleagues turned and politely congratulated me on 'my' composition. Wryneck even leaned over and told me I had 'reached the bounds of absolute music'.

Nonetheless, there was no denying that this was Greylag's evening. I allowed him to enjoy his brief period in the public gaze. Then, as the rapturous crowds departed, I went and joined him in the orchestra pit. The musicians were packing away their instruments.

'You can have a rest tomorrow,' I announced to all of them. 'Rest for as long as you wish.'

Then I spoke quietly to Greylag.

'I've got a treat in store for you tomorrow, Greylag,' I said. 'How would you like to go on a hike?'

'I'd like that very much, sir,' came the reply.

'All right,' I said. 'I'll call for you in the morning.'

Oddly enough, I didn't sleep very well that night. I should have enjoyed the luxurious slumber of success, but I didn't. Maybe it was the combined turmoil and excitement of the evening's performance that kept me awake; or perhaps it was the prospect of public unrest when Wryneck and Smew were unmasked. Besides these larger considerations there was also that shrill piping sound which Whimbrel and I had heard coming from the east. I kept hearing it again in my mind as I drifted off to sleep, and it was almost as if it was trying somehow to obliterate all trace of Greylag's music.

I met him in the half-light of early morning. He emerged from the cake wearing his usual black and scarlet frock coat and brass buckled boots. Clearly these were the only clothes he had. My plans for the hike were simple. I intended to head in the general direction of the plume of smoke. It didn't really matter if we failed to find its source, but we could at least try. In addition, there was plainly some sort of encampment out there, so that would be worth investigating too. At first when we set off Greylag kept walking a few paces behind me, as though he was my servant. Only after my repeated insistence that we travelled side by side did he at last comply.

'We're equals today, Greylag,' I said.

'Thank you, sir,' he replied.

The open air was very much a novelty for Greylag and he spent a lot of time 'taking in the sights'. In truth, there wasn't much to see. We wandered through the various postal districts before striking east into the hinterland beyond. Soon we were passing amongst brushwood and scrub, interspersed with marshes of reeds, rushes and sedge. There were fewer trees here than in the royal park; neither were there any footpaths to mark the way, though the proper wilderness still lay some miles ahead. Not that this seemed of any concern to Greylag. He was obviously delighting in every minute of his day out, so we just kept on going.

It was a mild day for the time of year, but I could tell that the weather in general was deteriorating. As we continued walking I wondered how long Wryneck and Smew had expected to bask in their glorious teatime sunsets. After all, the clocks could hardly be put forward in perpetuity; otherwise, every morning would eventually be lost in delayed darkness. Moreover, the sun was becoming increasingly pale by the day: even now it barely rose high enough to show its face through the gloom of late autumn. Judging by the sky there was little prospect of a decent sunset this evening, and I felt slightly sorry for Wryneck and Smew. At five o'clock (adjusted time) they would realise the futility of their deeds.

Meanwhile, the publication of counterfeit edicts had led them into very perilous territory. Even if they were acting for the good of the empire, which I didn't doubt, there would now be a question mark hanging over each of them. I was especially surprised at Wryneck, who had appeared so anxious to curb even minor instances of 'treason'. As for Smew, I'd long held the opinion that he was a vain and egotistical man. I wouldn't have put it past him if he'd taken the ceremonial crown for himself, even if it was only a gold-painted replica. From what I could gather, nobody knew where the real crown was. Presumably it was locked safely away somewhere, and the only person who might know its whereabouts was the emperor himself; except that he wasn't an emperor in the fully fledged sense because he'd never been crowned. He was a prince who for reasons of his own had failed to return from university. This in turn meant that Greater Fallowfields was not at present an empire. It wasn't even a kingdom: it was only a principality.

I was snapped out of my reverie by a shrill piping sound in the near distance.

Greylag stopped in his tracks and listened.

'G sharp,' he announced.

'Really?' I said.

More shrill piping followed.

'Definitely G sharp,' said Greylag. 'What a marvellously powerful instrument that must be.'

We resumed our hike. Ahead of us the scrub was starting to thicken into woodland. Further away lay great stands of forest, though I wasn't sure whether we would get that far. I could feel rain approaching. We decided to call a halt while it was still dry. Greylag and I sat down and shared some ship's biscuits that I'd obtained from Sanderling.

'I don't know for certain,' I said, nodding towards the east, 'but I think someone's building a railway out there.'

'Really, sir?' said Greylag. 'Is that allowed?'

'Probably not,' I said, 'but if they've managed to come this far the question is beside the point.'

Indeed, the matter of who was 'allowed' to do what in this region had never previously arisen. Apart from those few attempts at forestry, we had chosen to ignore the 'near east' in exactly the same way as we did the 'far east'. The wilderness had always been regarded as a natural frontier which therefore required no further development. It had evidently never occurred to anyone that there might be pioneers coming through from the other side. As Smew had mentioned in his recent talks, the empire assumed unceasingly that 'the rest of the world' could never impinge on our sphere of influence. He also seemed to suggest that there were some unspoken doubts surrounding this belief. Maybe, after all, he knew his subject better than I'd given him credit for.

The rain held off so we pressed forward. During the next hour we heard more shrill piping noises, as well as various clangs and hisses. Presently there also came the sound of men's voices. We passed some felled trees and entered a clearing. Shrouded in steam and smoke stood a huge, dark engine with a blackened funnel. Behind it an iron railway receded into the distance. A wire fence ran parallel on either side of the tracks. At the edge of the clearing was a double row of bell tents; also, some kind of field kitchen.

I had never seen men working as hard as those gathered around the engine. They barely glanced in our direction when we appeared out of the scrub, but just kept on labouring at their task. The sight of these men came as something of a revelation to me. We had a maxim in the empire:

HE SHALL EARN BUT A PENNY A DAY
BECAUSE HE CAN'T WORK ANY FASTER.

Or, more correctly, nobody worked faster than they needed to: not the postmen, nor the artisans, the clerks, or the purveyors of goods. That was how it had been as far back as I could remember. Even in the great days of shipping it often took equally as long to unload a vessel as it had for it to cross the sea in the first place. Such was the abundance that there was simply no need to hurry.

These men, by contrast, had clearly never heard the maxim. Or if they had they chose to pay it no attention. It was impossible to see what was driving them as they strove to lay their iron rails and move the engine, yard by yard, towards its destination. Every function was performed with the efficiency of clockwork. None of these men paused even for a moment's rest.

They were all attired in a plain olive drab uniform bearing a distinct insignia. This comprised the letters CoS.

After observing them for a minute or two I noticed that one man was standing slightly apart from the rest, and was giving instructions rather than physically working. When he saw Greylag and me he nodded as though he'd been expecting us. He issued a further set of instructions to his men; then he walked over to where we stood.

'I've been expecting a delegation,' he said. 'Is there any reason for the delay?'

Something in his tone suggested it would be unwise for me to admit I had no idea what he was talking about.

'Not as far as I know,' I replied.

'Well, I haven't got time to wait any longer,' he announced. 'I need to go back with the engine.'

He looked at his watch, then produced a whistle from his pocket and blew it twice. Immediately, the entire workforce downed tools and walked towards the engine. Within seconds another squad of men appeared from the direction of the tents. Having drawn closer I now saw that there was a windowless carriage attached to the rear of the engine. A sliding door was opened and the retiring men squeezed inside. Their replacements had already begun work when the engine repeated its shrill blast.

'All right,' said the man with the whistle, 'we'll no doubt meet again.'

He turned and strode briskly towards the engine.

'And you are?' I enquired.

'Gadwall,' he said, over his shoulder. 'Commissioner of Railways.'

He climbed into the carriage and blew his whistle once more. Then we watched as the great engine gathered steam and departed backwards down the track.

I was curious as to whether the remaining workers would ease their pace now that the overseer had departed. Or perhaps even cease work altogether, as would invariably be the practice in the empire. On the contrary these men continued without faltering, and again I wondered what unseen force could be propelling them. Meanwhile, the engine chugged and chuffed into the distance, the iron rails ringing forlornly beneath its wheels. Greylag seemed completely mesmerised by the sight and sound of these industrious men with their slavish engine. On his face was a faraway expression that I'd seen before. His eyes were glistening, just as they had been when I first outlined the requirements for the overture. Evidently he could detect music in the mechanical rumblings. The men themselves, of course, had no such 'romantic' notions. Their only interest was in laying the next set of rails. They laid them straight and level and then moved on, repeating the same process again and again. They took no notice of Greylag or me.

We gazed after the engine as gradually it diminished into a tiny speck. Moments before it vanished it gave a last shrill peep. Then it was heard no more.

15

'Which of you have done this?' demanded Garganey.

Certain changes had taken place during my brief absence. I'd only been away for one day yet in that time it appeared Garganey had seized power. He was standing at the far side of the room wearing the ceremonial crown. Everyone else was seated around the table, and I assumed I'd walked into an emergency meeting of the cabinet. It was only chance that had brought me here in the first place. I'd arrived home quite late in the evening and gone straight to bed. The following morning around ten o'clock I went to call on Whimbrel but found the observatory deserted. Guessing he must have gone to see Brambling about a replacement sixpence, I'd then proceeded to the counting house. Nobody was there either, so next I headed for the library. Maybe, I thought, Whimbrel or Brambling had some fact to look up in one of the books. It was Shrike who told me everyone was at the cabinet meeting. He'd been put temporarily in charge of the library and was plainly making the most of his new-found responsibility.

I discovered him lounging in Smew's comfortable chair by the large bay window. True enough, he jumped to his feet the instant he saw me. Nevertheless, it was obvious he'd been idling.

The clock had finished striking ten when I left the library and headed for the cabinet room. Now I felt most annoyed. Why, I wanted to know, had I not been informed of the situation?

I happened to arrive just as Whimbrel was going in. Normally I would have hailed him, but this morning I wasn't in the mood. Surely he of all people could have told me what was happening. He was supposed to be a friend. Then again, he'd recently been testing this so-called friendship to the limit. For a start he'd never bothered to repay the sixpence I'd lent him. Oh, I know he wasn't going to run away with it; he was only around the corner and, besides, he needed the sixpence more than I did. Yet it was the principle that mattered: at least he could have offered to repay it. Maybe that was why he spent more time with Brambling than with me. Another flaw had been revealed on the evening we visited the Maypole. On that occasion Whimbrel had invited Sanderling and me back to the observatory for a 'bottle or two' as he put it. Quite reasonably we'd both taken this to mean a bottle or two of fine wine, not dandelion-and-burdock as it turned out to be. I recalled that Sanderling had been particularly disappointed. Nor did I like the way Whimbrel and Brambling had conjectured that I was the emperor in disguise. They'd patently discussed me as if I was

148

an exhibit in a display cabinet. Finally, of course, Whimbrel had a marked tendency to hog the telescope instead of sharing it with other people.

I watched as he entered the cabinet room. Then, after waiting a moment, I followed him inside. I was still taking my seat when Garganey uttered his declamation.

'Which of you have done this?' he said again.

'Done what?' I asked.

I noticed that both Wryneck and Smew were staring at me intently. They had the same look about them as when I'd arrived unexpectedly at teatime a few days before. Indeed, they seemed slightly taken aback. Then I realised that it would have probably suited the pair of them if I'd missed the cabinet meeting. After all, I was the only person who knew about their sleight of hand.

Or was I?

I glanced at my colleagues, one by one, and tried to decide who knew what. Then it occurred to me that Garganey must have seized power under this very pretext. He certainly looked enraged.

'Which of you have done this?' he repeated for the third time.

'What, my good lord?' said Wryneck.

At last, I thought, Wryneck was beginning to face up to the questions. If only Smew would break his stony silence then the whole issue could most likely be sorted out before lunch. What did he hope to gain by prolonging the deceit?

'Thou canst not say I did it,' declared Garganey.

'Did what?' I asked.

Garganey sat down at the table, removed the crown and put his head in his hands.

'It's no good,' he said. 'I can't do it any longer. I've tried my best and I've obviously failed.'

'Well, shall I do it then?' offered Smew.

'If you like,' said Garganey. 'You've coveted the crown long enough. You may as well take it for yourself.'

'The crown is no more than a hollow golden ring,' rejoined Smew, 'and kingship a mere feather in a man's cap.'

A murmur of assent passed around the table.

'All the same,' I said, 'someone's got to wear the crown, haven't they?'

'Naturally,' said Wryneck.

His voice was wary. Smew said nothing.

'I mean to say,' I continued, 'you can't have an empire without an emperor. It's even more ridiculous than an empire without any ships.'

'Or an empire without a proper telescope,' added Whimbrel.

'Precisely,' I said.

I was pleasantly surprised by Whimbrel's sudden ride to my rescue. I'd swum into much deeper water than I intended and I almost regretted speaking out. Still, it was too late now. The unclaimed crown remained at the centre of the table. Neither Wryneck, nor Smew, nor Garganey seemed prepared to pursue the matter any further. Not for the moment at least. In the event it was Brambling who spoke next.

'Sorry,' he said, 'did you say *without* an emperor?'

'Yes,' I affirmed, 'I did.'

Again I surveyed the faces around the table. All my colleagues were apparently engaged in thoughts of their own. Dotterel was studying his textbook closely; Whimbrel was gazing at the clock; Garganey, Wryneck and Smew were all looking at the ceremonial crown; Sanderling was staring vaguely at a portrait of a former emperor; and Brambling was peering at me. I was about to attempt some kind of explanation when Wryneck broke the silence.

'It seems the bird has flown the nest,' he announced.

'Oh,' said Brambling, 'I see.'

'You mean he's not here?' said Whimbrel.

'Correct.'

'Does this have anything to do with the dancing girls,' enquired Sanderling, 'the ones who became great with child?'

'It's quite possible,' replied Wryneck.

'I thought as much,' said Sanderling.

'Well, Wryneck,' I remarked, 'you should be congratulated on your opacity.'

'Thank you,' he said.

Dotterel glanced up from his book.

'Well if the bird's flown the nest,' he said, 'why on earth did he bother issuing those preposterous edicts?'

'The folly of youth,' said Smew.

'More to the point,' I said, 'how are we going to resolve the succession?'

'There's only one answer,' said Wryneck.

'Which is?'

'A regency.'

Without a further word he raised the crown and placed it on Smew's head.

16

NOTICE:

TO MARK THE OCCASION OF THE TWELVE–DAY FEAST

MR GALLINULE'S COMPANY OF STROLLING PLAYERS WILL

PERFORM A TRAGEDY

AT THE MAYPOLE.

THE COMPANY COMPRISES:

MR ORTOLAN

MR PUKEKA

MR ROSELLA

MR MITTERIA

MR CHIURLO

MR PENDULINE

MR MESTOLONE

AND

MR GALLINULE

EARLY BOOKING IS ADVISED

During the following week these printed posters began to appear all over the royal quarter. I had no idea how Gallinule managed to gain access to a printing press, but these days his resourcefulness never failed to surprise me.

Moreover, word had reached the cabinet that the strolling players were rehearsing the very same play as we were. It was generally agreed that they would make a better job of it than us. Consequently, Smew's first decision as regent was to abandon our amateur production and hand full responsibility to the professionals. As a gesture of goodwill a further loan of half-a-crown was granted to Gallinule's company, the payment to be made from the exchequer. When Brambling protested about this, Wryneck intervened to explain that the sum involved could be shown in the books as a 'balancing figure'.

'Balanced against what?' asked Brambling.

'Itself,' said Wryneck. 'The original subvention can be regarded as a disallowable claim upon the state. The cancelled amount can therefore be brought forward and balanced against the current debt.'

'Oh,' said Brambling, 'I see.'

'That's agreed then,' said Smew.

He was sitting in the previously unoccupied emperor's chair. On his head he wore the ceremonial crown.

I had expected Garganey and Dotterel to raise the loudest voices against Smew's assumption of power. In fact, though, they both seemed to have accepted the new regime as a lesser evil. Perhaps they thought it would be easier to deal directly with Smew than with an unapproachable emperor. Even so, they made it clear what their priorities were:

'Surely there are more important matters to discuss than Gallinule's financial affairs,' said Dotterel, at the first meeting of the 'regency' cabinet. 'We really must sort out this question of the clocks.'

Dotterel had a point, of course. The cabinet had met at ten in the morning, yet we'd all had to find our way there in fading darkness. At five in the evening the sun would set unwitnessed behind masses of dark clouds. Winter was almost upon us and there were precious few hours of daylight available. This was evidenced by reports from Garganey's postmen. They had no objection, they said, to rising from their beds before dawn. Actually, they were quite accustomed to such demands and recognised them as part of their job. The persistent gloom, however, was causing some postmen to lose their way. They complained of 'disorientation'. Accordingly, even more letters were going astray than usual. Meanwhile, Dotterel's artisans were spending so much time adjusting the clocks that all their other duties were being left unattended to.

'The imperial gates are meant to be painted once a year,' he said, as an example, 'but so far they remain untouched.'

Furthermore, it was becoming clear that the populace in general disapproved of the five o'clock sunset. They preferred the gradual descent into darkness that traditionally signalled the approach of the twelve-day feast. True enough, they were getting plenty of darkness as things stood, but they wanted it in the afternoons, not in the mornings.

With these thoughts in mind, the cabinet unanimously agreed to revoke the offending edict. Whimbrel was given the task of calculating exactly what time it would be if the clocks hadn't been altered. Then a date was chosen for the 'great readjustment' and a public half-holiday proclaimed by way of recompense. As Wryneck observed, it was the least we could do. The cabinet quickly voted these measures through and by the end of the meeting we were feeling very pleased with ourselves.

Only later did it occur to me that maybe I should have mentioned the railway. After all, its rapid encroachment was bound to affect life in the empire just as surely as the episode of the clocks. I was reminded of it on my next visit to the orchestra. I'd decided it was high time I dropped in on Greylag, whom I hadn't seen since our foray to the edge of the wilderness. As I neared the cake there suddenly came an extraordinary sound from within. It was very like the shrill piping we'd heard in the east, and for an instant I thought the railway engine was inside the building. This was impossible, of course, so I listened again and realised that what I could hear wasn't the exact sound but rather an impression of it.

After a few moments it ceased and silence returned. I opened the door and entered the auditorium. Down in the orchestra pit I could see the musicians having one of their pauses for reflection. They were talking quietly to one another and attending to their instruments. In the meantime, Greylag sat at the piano plinking odd notes and making alterations to a manuscript. Nobody had noticed my arrival so I found a seat in the back row and watched. After a while Greylag went to the podium and gave some instructions to the orchestra. Then he held his baton aloft before quickly bringing it down again. Gradually he spread his arms outwards and the sound returned, distantly at first but steadily drawing nearer, then rising up in a great single chord. It immediately conjured up the railway engine, but now transmitted through ninety-eight musical instruments! Yet at the same time there was something else as well. The chord Greylag had created contained not only an industrial shrillness, but also a kind of sad cry. It was as if he had attributed feelings to this mechanical beast.

Eventually Greylag gave another signal and the music stopped. Then he returned to the piano and began making further adjustments. To me it sounded perfect already, but I had come to know that for Greylag perfection was unattainable. It was evident he was wholly absorbed in his work, so quietly I left the auditorium and went outside.

Darkness had fallen, but for some reason I wandered into the royal park and began roaming amongst the ancient trees. I quite liked their timeless presence, especially on winter evenings when the wind roared through the empty branches. Some distance away I could see the lights of the observatory tower. These told me that Whimbrel was at home, and I made my mind up to call on him later. Oddly enough, however, I thought I saw some other lights moving amid the trees. I remained standing where I was, and the lights drew closer. Finally, two figures appeared out of the gloom. The first I

157

recognised as Mestolone. The second, who I did not know, was carrying a torch.

'How does the night?' he asked.

'The moon is down,' replied Mestolone. 'I have not heard the clock.'

'And she goes down at twelve,' said the other man.

They obviously hadn't noticed me standing there in the shadows, and for a few moments I listened with interest as they continued discussing how dark it was. Then I deliberately stepped on a dead branch that was lying nearby.

'Who's there?' they said.

'Only me,' I answered. 'I was on my way up to the observatory when I heard you coming.'

'Ah, good evening,' said Mestolone. 'I don't think you've met Ortolan?'

I was introduced to the other actor, and Mestolone enquired if I would be coming to see their play when it was ready.

'Certainly,' I said. 'I'm looking forward to witnessing a professional performance.'

'It's sixpence a ticket,' said Mestolone.

Just then another light approached through the trees.

'Who's there?' said Ortolan.

'A friend,' said a voice, and presently Gallinule emerged from the darkness. He, too, was carrying a torch.

What most caught my attention, though, was the golden crown he had perched on his head. I could only see it dimly by the light of the torch, but it looked very similar to the ceremonial crown recently adopted by Smew.

'What, sir, not yet at rest?' said Ortolan.

Gallinule was about to reply when I interrupted.

'Yes, Mr Gallinule,' I said, 'I'd have thought you'd be ensconced in the Maypole by now.'

I only meant this as a friendly jest, but Gallinule seemed quite indignant.

'We players don't spend all our time drinking,' he said. 'We also have to rehearse.'

'Sorry,' I said. 'I forgot.'

Actually it was fairly easy to win back Gallinule's favour. I'd discovered soon after meeting him that all I needed to do was ask him a few questions about himself and he'd be happy. The trick worked again tonight. Soon he was telling me about all the important roles he'd performed during his career, and which particular part he had chosen for the forthcoming production. Naturally, it was the title role.

'Ah yes,' I said. 'Garganey had a go at playing him.'

'Had a go?' retorted Gallinule. 'One can't merely "have a go" at him: he speaks the greatest lines ever written!'

'Agreed,' I said quickly, 'and I'm sure you'll deliver them par excellence.'

This evidently satisfied Gallinule because next thing I was being invited to accompany the players to the Maypole that evening.

'I'd like to join you,' I said, 'but unfortunately the publican won't accept my stipendiary sixpence.'

This was technically true, though I failed to mention my pockets were empty.

'Oh, don't worry about the publican,' said Gallinule. 'We're running a slate at the Maypole.'

'You mean you get your beer on tick?'

'And wine, of course,' said Gallinule, 'depending on the time of day.'

'But I thought the slate was only for commoners.'

'We can play the commoner when required,' he said. 'We can also play the clown, the deluded lover, the madman and the hurt hawk, but our speciality is the royal roles. We are the Player King.'

The conversation continued to revolve around Gallinule as the four of us made our way towards the Maypole. Soon the remaining actors caught us up and I was introduced to Pukeka, Rosella, Mitteria, Chiurlo and Penduline. They were undoubtedly a colourful bunch and all plainly of the same ilk; by the time we entered the premises I was being treated as a lifelong friend. Accordingly, the publican's welcome was extended to include me.

As a matter of fact I discovered that we officers-of-state were now held in high esteem by the general populace. Word was out that the 'conspiracy of the clocks' had been foiled thanks to our resolve; and everyone was looking forward to the long, dark evenings of the twelve-day feast. Trade at the Maypole had increased already. My first pint, therefore, was 'on the house'. The players and I sat around a long table and revelled in good cheer. Over in the corner the postmen were playing a game of dominoes. From somewhere else there came an occasional snatch of song. I gazed at my foaming beer glass,

160

the sea of smiling faces and the blazing log fire, and decided I could probably come to enjoy such a life.

There was only one disappointment.

'You should have been here last night, really,' announced Gallinule. 'They had a bevy of dancing girls.'

He was still wearing his golden crown, and only removed it when Mestolone reminded him.

'Force of habit,' said Gallinule. 'We've been rehearsing all day and I quite forgot.'

He placed the crown on the table.

'Do you mind if I try it on?' I said.

Gallinule had no objection, so I lifted the crown and weighed it in my hands. It was evidently a lightweight model just the same as Smew's. In fact, under the bright lights I could see that it was identical. Briefly I put it on my head, and when I took it off again I happened to glance inside the rim. There I saw a small insignia which I assumed to be the mark of the maker. On closer examination it turned out to comprise the letters CoS.

'Where did you get this?' I asked.

'Oh, we likely picked it up on our travels,' replied Gallinule. 'It's only a stage prop.'

'Actually,' said Mestolone, 'it was left behind when our king went into exile.'

'Really?' I said.

'We saved it from falling into the wrong hands,' he added.

'Well, it's still worthless,' said Gallinule. 'Base metal and gold paint.'

I looked at Mestolone and noticed he had that same sad expression on his face I'd seen once before. I began to wish I hadn't asked about the provenance of the crown. I also realised that he differed from the rest of the troupe somewhat. They were all born actors, while he was a handyman who did some acting when needed. His true place was behind the scenes and he had little interest in the limelight.

Unlike Gallinule, of course, who even made a performance of ordering a round of drinks.

'We need recourse to your bounteous munificence,' he declared on his next visit to the counter. The star-struck publican dutifully filled our glasses and Gallinule returned triumphant.

As the evening passed, however, it occurred to me that as an officer-of-state I needed to show some self-restraint. There appeared to be no limit to the slate that Gallinule was running up, and for all I knew we could be drinking until dawn. For this reason I decided that I would have four pints and then leave. When the time eventually came my new-found companions voiced all sorts of protests, and demanded promises that I would join them again the following evening, and made further pledges of everlasting friendship. Only after every conceivable bond had been forged was I allowed to leave. They bade me a last hearty farewell and I departed into the night.

Outside, everything felt different. I had no idea what time it was but the streets were completely deserted so I guessed it was very late. Many of the lights had gone out, and those that were still lit had a rather cold glow about them. Fortunately the moon was shining brightly, a fact which seemed a little odd to me, though I couldn't think why. I looked left, then right, then left again, pondering which way to go before finally choosing neither course. I crossed over and walked straight up the street opposite. Then I turned a corner. Then another. By now I wasn't thinking about where I was going. Nor was I looking back on the wonderful evening I'd enjoyed. I was just walking. After a while I found myself in the park, stumbling along amongst the trees. They looked stark and sombre in the moonlight. The wind was still roaring through their branches and I stopped to listen for a minute. As I stood there swaying I saw a lamp glowing in the observatory. Whimbrel was obviously still at work so I resolved to call in on him. It took some time to find my way to the start of the curving path, but I traipsed on and ultimately arrived at his door.

I knocked and waited; then knocked and knocked again.

'Hold on,' I heard him cry from above, 'I'm coming.'

He made me wait an hour before opening the door.

'What kept you?' I said.

'Give me a chance,' he replied. 'I got down as quick as I could.'

'I've come to pay you a visit,' I announced.

'Yes, so I see.' He shone his lamp in my face. 'Are you feeling all right?'

'Of course,' I said, 'never better.'

'Well, I think you ought to come in.'

Whimbrel's tone suggested I wasn't quite myself. He led me up the iron spiral and sat me down in a chair. Then he gave me a glass of water. He watched me sternly for a moment or two, then went to his chart table and resumed his work. How long I remained sitting there I don't know, but every time I looked across at Whimbrel he was still examining his charts. After a while I asked him for another glass of water and gradually I began to feel normal again. I didn't move, though, and continued gazing idly at Whimbrel as he worked.

'What are you doing?' I enquired at length.

'I'm trying to calculate what time it is,' he answered, 'so that the clocks can be readjusted.'

'I thought you finished that hours ago.'

'It's proving more difficult than I expected,' said Whimbrel. 'To tell you the truth I don't even know where to start.'

'Well, how did you manage before?'

'It was different then,' he explained. 'The clocks were all correct. Now they're all wrong.'

Whimbrel sounded desperate. All those charts and tables he had at his disposal were apparently of no use at all. Not when he couldn't understand them, anyway.

'If it's any help,' I said, 'the moon goes down at twelve.'

'Does it?' replied Whimbrel.

'So maybe you could work it out from there.'

'Yes,' he said, his mood suddenly brightening.

I heaved myself out of my chair and the two of us went over to the window. Sure enough, there was the moon, shining in all its glory. It was about to dip over the horizon.

164

'Just in time,' I remarked.

'What a piece of good luck,' said Whimbrel. 'Thank heavens you turned up when you did. You've saved the day.'

'Night,' I said.

We spent the next few minutes eagerly following the slow descent of the moon. Whimbrel stood next to his clock, and at the required moment he altered the hands to midnight. Then he got to work producing a new set of tables. I assisted by tearing up the old ones.

'By the way,' he said, 'remember that shrill piping noise we heard in the east?'

'Oh, yes?' I replied.

'Well I've been hearing it again recently, and it seems to be much closer than before.'

'It's only the orchestra,' I said. 'Greylag is experimenting.'

'Is that allowed?' Whimbrel asked.

'Certainly,' I answered. 'I've given him a free hand following his success with the overture. He's very interested in the musical undertones of industrial progress.'

'Good grief,' said Whimbrel. 'How on earth does he know about that?'

'He just does,' I said with a shrug. 'Greylag is much more than a simple serf, you know. As a matter of fact I'm convinced he's a genius.'

At these words, Whimbrel turned away from his tables and gave me a penetrating look. 'Then don't you think it's time you did something for him?'

'What sort of something?' I said.

'Well,' said Whimbrel, 'you could use your influence to help him gain freedom from bondage.'

For a few moments I stared at Whimbrel with surprise.

'Yes, I suppose I could,' I said. 'I never thought of that.'

We continued labouring over Whimbrel's tables for several hours more. He was keen to get them completed as soon as possible so that he could present them to the cabinet as a *fait accompli*. After that he intended to go to the royal printing works and get them published throughout the empire. It was almost light when at last we finished. Considering the season, dawn came much sooner than we expected. According to the clock it was only half past five, yet daylight was already starting to stream in through the windows. Nonetheless, we both agreed that the time must be correct. We were committed to the new tables: there was no going back now.

Whimbrel cooked breakfast and thanked me for my help; then I set off on a brisk morning walk. I needed to clear my head and the park was the perfect setting. My plan was to take a stroll around the boating lake. I hadn't got very far, however, when I heard the familiar shrill piping. It was rather early in the day, I thought, for Greylag to be at work. Besides which, the sound was coming not from the cake but from another direction entirely. Soon I heard it again. Quickly I crossed the park to the gates at the far side. Then I walked through the outlying postal districts. After half an hour I arrived at the edge of the capital. There amongst the scrub and brush stood the railway engine. The track, it seemed, was complete. I approached cautiously and saw Gadwall overseeing the final operation. A pair of buffers was being placed in position by his gang of men.

When he saw me he was polite and we exchanged greetings.

'Congratulations,' I said. 'It looks like a fine piece of workmanship.'

'Thank you,' he replied.

We watched as the last nuts and bolts were fastened. Then the engine gave a shrill whistle. The job was truly finished.

'Is this the end of the line?' I asked.

'No,' said Gadwall, 'this is the beginning.'

17

Later that morning an emergency meeting of the cabinet was convened. It was supposed to be a half-holiday: the occasion when the clocks were readjusted and 'proper' imperial time resumed. Indeed, Dotterel's artisans had already begun the painstaking task of converting Whimbrel's calculations into reality. All over the capital, clocks were being carefully altered. Meanwhile, Garganey's postmen delivered the instructions further afield. When they returned, it was proposed, the half-holiday could commence.

At some point, however, word had reached Smew about the arrival of the railway. Accordingly, we were all summoned to the cabinet room.

'Why weren't we informed?' Smew demanded. 'Someone has built a railway right up to our doorstep yet nobody noticed.'

'Well, my artisans have been far too busy with the clocks,' said Dotterel. 'They hardly had time for anything else.'

'My postmen have been stumbling around in darkness,' added Garganey. 'We can't blame them either.'

Smew turned to Whimbrel. 'What about you?' he said. 'Didn't you see anything through your telescope?'

'Wait a minute,' I interjected. 'It's not Whimbrel's fault. He only gets one sixpence at a time.'

'Besides which,' said Whimbrel, 'I'm supposed to be looking at the stars, not the approach of railways.'

'Quarrelling isn't going to get us anywhere,' said Dotterel. 'Shouldn't we decide what we're going to do?'

'Agreed,' said Wryneck.

'One fact is for certain,' said Smew. 'We don't need a railway.'

A murmur of assent passed around the table.

'This empire was built on seafaring,' he continued. 'We have always travelled by ship and no other means of transport are required. A railway will only bring unwelcome influences.'

'Such as?' I asked.

'The customs of the east,' said Smew. 'We don't want them here.'

'But doesn't the railway represent progress?' said Dotterel. 'Resisting it would be like trying to stop the tide from turning.'

'Progress doesn't bring improvement,' declared Smew. 'It just makes people think they're cleverer than they actually are.'

'We can't have that,' said Wryneck.

'Of course we can't,' said Smew.

'What I want to know,' said Garganey, 'is how they had the audacity to build this railway without consulting us?'

'I imagine,' said Smew, 'that it's the product of a so-called friendly city: the kind I discussed in my recent talks. Here we see a typical example of the way they operate. They simply drive forward, meeting each obstruction as it comes. It seems that one such city is flourishing particularly well at the moment. History suggests it will be at the expense of others.'

'Not us, though, surely?' said Whimbrel.

'As long as we're vigilant, no,' replied Smew, 'but we need to consider our options carefully.'

'Why don't we send a delegation?' I said. 'Then we could speak with the railwaymen and find out their intentions.'

'That would be an indication of weakness,' said Wryneck. 'Far better if we wait until they come to us.'

'Agreed,' said Smew. 'We must carry on as normal and make it clear that their presence will have no effect on our way of life.'

During the course of the meeting the sky had been darkening steadily. A glance at the clock told me it was half past twelve. There was no sign of rain, yet the light continued to deteriorate. It then occurred to me that the descending murk had nothing to do with the weather: what I was witnessing was the onset of dusk. Nobody else appeared to notice, however, so I didn't say anything.

There was a knock on the door and Shrike came in. He approached Smew and bowed. 'The post has arrived, my liege.'

There was only one item: a letter in a brown envelope bearing an unusual postmark. Smew opened it.

'Confounded cheek!' he exclaimed. 'They've sent an invoice for the construction of the railway.'

'Well, we're not paying it,' uttered Brambling. 'The imperial funds aren't for white elephants.'

Smew was still peering at the invoice. 'I'm afraid we may not have any choice,' he said. 'Apparently the order was signed by the emperor himself.'

We all gasped in disbelief.

'Well he might at least have told us!' snapped Dotterel.

'Maybe he did,' said Whimbrel. 'Perhaps his letter was lost in the post.'

Everybody looked at Garganey, as though this was all somehow his fault.

'Don't blame me,' he said. 'The emperor's landed us with this railway when we didn't even ask for one.'

'If you don't ask you don't get,' said Sanderling.

During this discussion, Shrike had been waiting patiently in the corner of the room. Now, having observed the turmoil caused by the invoice, he quietly departed.

'We shouldn't argue in front of the serfs,' I said. 'It doesn't look very good at all.'

'Actually, Shrike is no longer a serf,' said Smew. 'I've had him raised to a commoner.'

Smew made this announcement in a very lofty tone of voice. He was sitting in the emperor's chair, and as usual displayed all the confidence of a natural ruler.

'May we take it that you intend to continue as regent?' asked Garganey.

'Correct,' said Smew. He handed the invoice to Brambling. 'Your department, I believe.'

Brambling examined the figures and his eyes widened.

'Good grief,' he said. 'I'll need to trawl the coffers.'

On Wryneck's suggestion, Brambling was dispatched to the counting house to do some reckoning. Meanwhile, the rest of the cabinet agreed that we would play a waiting game.

'If they want money they're going to have to come and get it,' concluded Smew.

Darkness had fallen by the time our deliberations were over. Nobody passed comment that it was still only three in the afternoon, and I therefore assumed everyone was quite satisfied with the 'new' hours. The temptation, of course, was to head directly for the Maypole where the lights would be glowing and the log fire roaring. Indeed, the place was thronging when I passed it by. The twelve-day feast was almost upon us and the people were clearly getting in the mood. Nevertheless, I had a more important matter on my mind. The pleasures of the Maypole would have to wait.

I wanted to look into this question of Greylag's freedom, so I went to the library and perused the bookshelves. Smew's revelation that Shrike had been raised to a commoner was encouraging, but actually I thought Greylag deserved better. Eventually I found what I was seeking: the correct term in Greylag's case was 'manumission'. According to the records, a serf granted manumission would become a freeman, a step above mere commoners in the feudal system. This, I decided, was what I should try and strive towards.

I drifted into the reading room and noticed that Smew had left his crown unattended on the desk by the bay window. I picked it up and glanced inside the rim. It came as no surprise to see the letters CoS stamped there.

'Probably an import,' said a voice behind me.

I turned to see Dotterel standing in the doorway.

'A cheap one at that,' I remarked.

'I expect it came in from the east,' he said. 'Not directly, though. It most likely found its way here via the colonies.'

The crown felt tinny and insubstantial in my hands. Casually I tossed it over to Dotterel.

'Rather careless of Smew to leave it lying around,' he said. 'I've a good mind to confiscate it.'

'On what grounds?' I asked.

'On the grounds that I'm custodian of the imperial arte-facts,' he said. 'In the last resort I'm responsible for the upkeep of this crown: that's why it was in the royal workshop in the first place.'

He began buffing up the crown with his handkerchief.

'We had to straighten all the prongs,' he continued, 'and apply a new coat of gold paint. In terms of time spent it would have been much cheaper to get a replacement.'

'Couldn't they make a new one,' I suggested, 'in the workshop?'

Dotterel shook his head. 'We don't make anything in this country,' he said. 'Not any more. We just carry out repairs.'

He put the gleaming crown back on the desk.

'That's better,' he said.

'Did you come here especially to give it a polish?' I enquired.

'Actually, no,' said Dotterel. 'I wanted to return this.'

He reached into his pocket and produced a textbook.

'It's the play we've been rehearsing,' he explained. 'I won't need it now.'

He went to the bookshelves and put it back with the other copies.

'You know Smew was wrong?' he said. 'The king was the only person who could see the ghost, not the other way round.'

'Yes,' I agreed, 'and he wasn't a king, he was a usurper.'

'Smew's judgement is far from perfect.'

'What about the railway?' I said. 'Do you think he's wrong about that too?'

'Entirely wrong,' replied Dotterel. 'You can't stop progress.'

He took a last look at the crown, then wished me good evening and departed. After that I spent quite some time moping around the library while I pondered the situation. Privately I hoped Dotterel's assessment was incorrect, but I knew deep down that it wasn't.

By the following day the railway had become public knowledge. As a matter of fact it was quickly turning into a tourist attraction. The first I knew of it was when I approached the park and saw streams of people heading eastward. I'd planned to call in on Greylag and tell him my intentions for achieving his freedom from bondage. In view of the roaming hordes, however, I decided to find out the cause of all the fuss. Besides which, on second thoughts it seemed a shame to raise Greylag's hopes too early. Far better to surprise him with some good news later. With this in mind I bypassed the cake and joined the milling crowd.

It was soon obvious where we were all going. We took the same route to the edge of the capital as I had the day before. Ultimately we came to the railway, which now had a brand-new platform running alongside it. Once again the work had been completed at a remarkable speed. This was something I'd come to expect just lately. What I didn't anticipate, however, was the total absence of a train. Gadwall and his men had left the place deserted. The only draw for sightseers was an empty platform, a pair of buffers, and a set of iron rails diminishing into the distance.

My attention was caught by a noticeboard at the far end of the platform. On closer inspection I found that it displayed a timetable for the forthcoming railway service. Then, to my irritation, I saw that all the arrivals and departures were listed in 'local time'.

The effrontery of these people! Not only had they built a railway without due consultation, but now they were suggesting that the time in Greater Fallowfields was merely 'local'. This implied that the time elsewhere was more important! Clearly, they hadn't allowed for the recent adjustments we'd been making to our clocks, nor did they appear the slightest bit interested.

No less disquieting was the series of letters printed in the right-hand column of the timetable. These letters represented the scheduled destination for every train, and in each case they were identical: CoS.

As I stood gazing at the noticeboard I reflected that Gadwall and his companions were not entirely to blame for the advent of the railway. Our uncrowned emperor had played his part too. Presumably he'd signed the order as some sort of student prank while he was far away at university. No wonder he was reluctant to return home and face the music! Recently a number of other theories had been put forward to excuse his continued absence. Prevalent among these was the suggestion that he was probably studying hard for his exams. This struck me as spurious to say the least: it was a historical fact that the young emperors seldom returned with any kind of qualification.

Sanderling, of course, had a far simpler explanation. He remained convinced that it was all to do with the dancing girls who'd suddenly vanished from court. He mentioned them almost every time I saw him; or else the dancing girls from the Maypole; or the dancing girls he'd heard about from various marooned admirals with whom he was acquainted. Poor Sanderling! He lived in a world of self-delusion. He assumed there were dancing girls hidden around every corner, but he was yet to meet them.

I was still contemplating all this when I became aware of a swell of expectation passing through the crowd. Many people were now lining the railway on either side, and as I listened

I heard a familiar shrill piping sound. It was only faint at first, but gradually it grew louder. I leaned over the edge of the platform and peered down the track. Sure enough, in the distance I saw a dark plume of smoke. Below it loomed the approaching train. The smoke was rising in puffs, and with each puff the engine panted as though labouring under a great weight. Evidently it was slowing down at the end of a long journey: I could hear the iron wheels grinding on the rails; and as the noise grew louder the onlookers began chattering more loudly too. A bell started clanging. The formidable engine was now bearing down upon the multitude, causing those standing nearest the track to step back a pace. Hence a wobbly line of people marked the progress of the train. The shrill whistle was repeated. Then the brakes squealed and the puffing ceased. The engine drew alongside the platform and halted. Attached behind it were half a dozen windowless carriages. There were ventilation slits above the sliding doors, and one by one these doors began to open. The first to emerge was Gadwall. He was followed by a number of his men in their plain olive drab uniforms. The assembled spectators had long since fallen silent; meanwhile the engine continued to hiss and groan. Gadwall looked down the platform and saw me in my dandy coat.

'Aha,' he said, 'an imperial reception.'

The majority of those present were commoners. They'd taken little notice of me during the rush to see the new railway, and I'd been more or less swept along in their wake. I'd literally become one of the herd, despite my distinguished appearance.

This was typical of the general public when they turned out for a popular event. They only saw what they wanted to see. They'd have been quite unaware if the emperor himself was standing in their midst, let alone an officer-of-state, such was their single-minded fervour.

Now, however, they seemed completely overawed by the sight of the newcomers, and it required someone of my calibre to take the reins. Unfortunately, I was constrained by the cabinet's recent injunction. We had agreed unanimously not to make any sort of approach to the railwaymen. My present visit was in a strictly personal capacity and therefore I needed to maintain a low profile.

A brief hiatus ensued, during which Gadwall looked at me and I looked at him. Then suddenly there was a nearby kerfuffle. I glanced around and saw Gallinule advancing through the throng in his finest crimson apparel. Without so much as a nod in my direction he spoke directly to Gadwall.

'Gallinule at your service,' he said. 'May we introduce our company?'

In a veritable *coup de théâtre* he then proceeded to introduce Ortolan, Pukeka, Rosella, Mitteria, Chiurlo and Penduline. (Mestolone was nowhere to be seen.)

Gadwall regarded the entourage in solemn silence for several moments. They were attired in all manner of outlandish clothing, yet his face betrayed neither astonishment nor curiosity.

'What is your business?' he enquired.

'The world, sir, is our business,' replied Gallinule.

'Then you may wish to attend one of our pavilions,' said Gadwall. 'As you can see, preparations are already under way.'

Indeed, the preparations Gadwall referred to were going on apace. Within minutes of arriving the men in olive drab had begun unloading the carriages. In a highly organised operation out came boxes, crates and large bundles of fabric. Very soon a site had been cleared and rows of bell tents erected. These appeared to be for purposes of accommodation, but beyond them some much larger tents were gradually being hoisted into position.

A good part of the crowd had started slowly to disperse, having evidently lost interest after the train's glorious arrival. A substantial number remained, however, and they seemed almost mesmerised by the frenetic activity they were witnessing. Such industriousness was seldom seen in Greater Fallowfields, and for some it was plainly a fascinating spectacle. Gallinule and his colleagues had soon embarked on a guided tour of the new encampment. In the meantime I decided to take the opportunity to slip quietly away. Privately I suspected Gallinule was on the verge of becoming unstuck. It was obvious to me that he'd only come along to test the market for theatre tickets. Somehow, though, he'd managed to convince Gadwall that he was a man of local importance; and he was now being entertained accordingly. I had no doubt that his acting abilities would enable him to wriggle out of any impending situation, but I didn't want to be involved.

I wandered along the platform, peering casually through each carriage doorway as I passed. Some interiors were stacked full of equipment; others were virtually empty. The final carriage, I noticed, was not included in all the hustle and bustle. The men in olive drab uniforms did not venture near, and nothing was being unloaded. Nonetheless, I sensed that there was somebody inside.

As I drew near a man appeared in the doorway and looked out. He, too, was dressed in olive drab, but his demeanour was somehow different from the others. There was a certain stillness about him as he observed the unflagging toil of his compatriots. When he saw me coming he directed his gaze at me. I perceived straight away that he was carrying out a visual assessment: it was almost as if he was deducing my worth from my physical appearance. In other words, he was weighing me up.

Then he beckoned me over and spoke. 'Give me a hand here, will you?'

I glanced into the carriage and saw behind him a large wooden trunk with brass handles at each end. Evidently he had misjudged me: it was quite obvious he thought I was some kind of court functionary who would jump at his every command. Or perhaps he even took me for the station porter! Either way, I decided to play along with the whole game. After all, there was no harm in offering help to a newly arrived traveller.

'Certainly,' I said, reaching in and grasping one of the handles.

Together we slid the trunk towards the doorway. Then, with a grunt or two, we heaved it down on to the platform.

A few seconds went by as I stood waiting in silence. An acknowledgement of some sort was all that was required, yet the man did not thank me for my assistance. Instead, to my surprise, he put a silver sixpence in the palm of my hand.

'There you are,' he said.

Naturally, I was flabbergasted. It was one thing to be mistaken for a servant, but entirely another to be treated as one. For a moment I gazed speechless at the man, who had already moved away and was attending to other business inside the carriage. It was plain that he regarded the transaction as a matter of course, while from my point of view it was practically an affront. Indeed, such conduct was unheard of throughout the empire.

On the other hand, it occurred to me that this unexpected turn of events could resolve an embarrassing problem at a stroke. Whimbrel had failed persistently to return the stipendiary sixpence I'd lent him. Moreover, I had no inclination to ask for it back. Now all of a sudden there was a sixpence lying in the palm of my hand. Here was a chance to receive recompense indirectly. Besides, it would be awkward trying to return the offering. In the next instant the man closed the carriage door, leaving me standing alone on the station platform. Without further debate I slipped the coin into my pocket and headed homewards.

Dusk was falling, although it was barely past midday. In the distance the lights of the capital were gradually beginning

181

to glow and there was a definite feeling of seasonal jollity in the air. I had to admit that I now felt fairly pleased with the outcome of my morning jaunt. Not only had I witnessed the arrival of the first scheduled train, but I'd also been fully reimbursed with my stipendiary sixpence. All at once I felt like an officer-of-state again. No longer was I dependent on Brambling's begrudged generosity: I now had a sixpence of my own!

As I continued walking I began to conjecture what the others did with their stipends. I knew that Whimbrel dutifully fed his sixpence into the observatory telescope, and I assumed Sanderling was saving his for when he finally tracked down those elusive dancing girls. I had no idea, however, about the spending habits of the remaining officers. I then fell to pondering whether Smew still claimed his official payment as librarian-in-chief. I concluded that he probably did, and that most likely he'd taken the liberty of raising it to a shilling, or maybe even half-a-crown. Such, he might argue, were the prerogatives of regency.

Meanwhile, I had no doubt that Wryneck kept his money in a piggy bank.

With these idle thoughts in mind I reached the outskirts of the royal quarter. What luck to be given a new sixpence on the eve of the twelve-day feast! I paused beneath a lamp post and removed the coin from my pocket. This was the first time I'd examined it properly and I was startled to discover that it wasn't a sixpence at all. Lying in the palm of my hand was a type of coin I'd never seen before. In size, weight and shape it was identical to an imperial sixpence. It even glimmered the same way in the lamplight. Nevertheless it was clearly something quite different. I held it nearer to the light and inspected it closely. The design was simple. On one side was a hammer and anvil; on the other were three words: CITY OF SCOFFERS.

18

When the first day of feasting arrived I realised I hadn't made any festive arrangements. I'd been so busy with the orchestra, the railway and so forth that I hadn't noticed it creeping up on me. Most of the populace, of course, had all manner of preparations in hand: windows were decorated with brightly coloured lights, doors were garlanded, log fires were kindled, plum puddings were mixed and gooseberry pies were baked. The objective was to eat, drink and be merry, and consequently the public houses were expecting to do a roaring trade.

I should add, though, that the twelve-day feast was actually a misnomer. Celebrations rarely extended beyond the third day; after that the holiday subsided into a kind of limbo as the supply of cakes and ale slowly dwindled and people contemplated returning to work. The only citizens who customarily took the full twelve days were the postmen, so I was surprised when a card was delivered that very first morning. The postman who brought it informed me that mine was the only call he'd made today; furthermore, he'd had to rise from his bed especially to make it. I pointed out that I'd also had to rise from my bed especially to answer his knock, but he seemed unimpressed. He wished me a 'fruitful feast' and went on his way, presumably in the direction of the Maypole.

After he'd gone I opened the card. It was from Smew. Apparently he was holding a grand reception from three until five in the afternoon. The venue was the reading room of the great library, and I was invited. This more or less eliminated the other possibility open to me; namely, that of joining Gallinule and his companions in their chosen hostelry. I could imagine the sort of day that lay ahead of them and it was not uninviting. The drink flowed unusually freely when Gallinule was 'in the chair', and a pleasant time was therefore guaranteed. At the back of my mind, though, was the question of finance. I could hardly show up at the Maypole with my newly acquired coin and try to get it past the publican. Also, I might be put under pressure to purchase a ticket for the company's forthcoming play. Once more the problem came down to money. The price was sixpence; and sixpence I didn't have. As much as I wanted to see this tragedy, I didn't savour the prospect of sitting in a pauper's seat.

I looked again at Smew's invitation and decided I had no alternative but to accept. Indeed, it struck me that it would have been churlish not to. Here I was, being invited to the most prestigious social event of the season, one that was likely to be the envy of many, yet I was considering giving it a miss! I chided myself for being so foolish and set about getting ready.

The card said three o'clock but I determined to make my entrance at half past. Turning up any earlier would have made it look as if I had nowhere else to go, aside from which I wanted to avoid the awkwardness of being first to arrive. As it happened I need not have worried: that particular honour fell upon Sanderling. At three thirty I walked into the reading room to find him attired in his smartest dandy coat, and doing his best to converse with Wryneck. I could see immediately that he was struggling. The two of them appeared to be discussing the numerous portraits hanging around the walls, but there was a very obvious distraction. Close by stood a table laden with glasses, all brimming with wine, and as yet untouched. Poor Sanderling was plainly undergoing a mild form of torture. I watched with interest as he nodded and concurred with Wryneck, all the time casting glances at the wine as though he feared it would suddenly vanish. Meanwhile, Wryneck explained each painting down to the last tiny detail, before steering his hapless pupil towards the next masterpiece, and then the one after that. I wondered how long Sanderling would be able to bear being deprived of the drink that was so near and yet so far. Soon Whimbrel joined me, quickly followed by Dotterel, Brambling and Garganey. These last three were slightly damp. It was now raining outside, apparently, as well as being dark and gloomy. Exactly why our ancestors established the feast at this dismal time of year I didn't know, but I presumed it was because they needed an excuse to stay indoors.

I glanced around at my companions and noticed that Dotterel seemed rather ill at ease. There was evidently something bothering him but I didn't get the chance to find out what. Next moment Smew emerged from within some inner sanctum wearing the ceremonial crown and looking unquestionably regal. He regarded the little gathering for some moments, and then spoke.

'Why, Wryneck,' he said, 'aren't you going to offer our guests some wine?'

'Ah, yes,' Wryneck answered, 'I was so absorbed with the royal paintings that I clean forgot.'

For some reason the wine glasses ranged along the table were of many different sizes. They stood there glowing under the chandelier and I thought they looked most enticing. The larger glasses were towards the back; the medium and small ones nearer the front.

'Like a drink, Sanderling?' said Wryneck.

'Yes, please,' came the reply.

Wryneck turned and selected the smallest glass and handed it to Sanderling. Whether he did it on purpose I couldn't tell, but I found I was unable to continue witnessing Sanderling's torment. Instead I joined a short queue comprising Dotterel, Garganey, Whimbrel and Brambling. Wryneck favoured us all with large measures, but for himself he chose a glass of equal size to the one he'd given Sanderling.

Smew waited gracefully until last.

The eight of us must have looked quite magnificent as we stood assembled in our courtly attire, each holding a glass of the empire's finest wine. Here we were, the very cream of imperial government, enjoying one another's company in a library of international renown. All the same I couldn't help thinking that there was some special element lacking from the occasion. To put it another way, there was no sense of allure-ment: no sparkle. I was unable to put my finger precisely on what we were missing, but the feeling persisted nonetheless.

I was then struck by an unrelated secondary thought. It occurred to me that we might all be expected to exchange gifts at some stage during the afternoon. A cold chill ran through me as I realised I'd made no provision for this whatsoever. Realistically, I couldn't envisage Dotterel or Garganey produc-ing a sackful of carefully wrapped parcels out of the blue. On the other hand, I would not have put it past Whimbrel to dis-tribute presents left, right and centre just for the sake of it. How embarrassing, then, to be unable to offer anything in return.

I was still considering my options when Dotterel cleared his throat and addressed Smew directly.

'Smew,' he said, 'there's a matter of great urgency which I think demands the immediate attention of the cabinet.'

'Not now, Dotterel,' said Smew.

'But it's most important.'

'Not now,' Smew repeated. 'It will have to wait.'

'You mean until tomorrow?' Dotterel enquired.

'I mean until after the twelve-day feast.'

'It can't wait twelve days!'

'Of course it can,' said Smew. He had adopted a kind yet masterful tone of voice. 'Nothing should be allowed to interrupt the festivities,' he continued. 'Affairs of state must be put to one side for the time being. So please, Dotterel, try to enjoy yourself and let's hear no more about it.'

'Very well,' conceded Dotterel, bowing his head slightly and accepting a second glass of wine.

This was provided by Shrike, who had appeared as if from nowhere carrying a tray of drinks. After serving Dotterel he began circulating amongst the rest of us, and this time I was glad to see Sanderling receive the biggest glass of all. The general conversation then became much more convivial. Even Dotterel seemed to overcome his disquietude, if only temporarily.

The paintings lining the walls were not all portraits. Some of them depicted maritime scenes from the history of the empire. Sanderling now seized the opportunity to demonstrate what he had learned during his time at the admiralty. One enormous canvas showed a flotilla of sailing ships, merchantmen by the look of them, beating along some wild shore in search of a safe harbour. Taking Wryneck by the sleeve, Sanderling guided him over to the picture and started explaining it to him. Cleverly, though, he made no attempt to talk about artistic technique: brushstrokes, light, colour, perspective and so forth. This would have led him straight out of his depth. Instead he described how a ship actually sailed, commencing from first principles.

'What you need to understand,' he began, 'is that the wind doesn't simply blow the ship along. Rather, the ship takes the wind and shapes it to its own requirements.'

Wryneck stood listening intently as Sanderling outlined the basic laws of sailing. Dotterel and Garganey also moved a little closer, clearly impressed by Sanderling's wealth of knowledge. It was a shame he had no ships with which to put it all into practice.

Whimbrel, Brambling and Smew, meanwhile, had become involved in a discussion about Smew's pencil, which he always carried with him. He was well known for preferring pencils to pens, and now he explained the reason why.

'The mark of a pencil is softer and less intrusive,' he announced. 'Moreover, it can be rubbed out. Ink on the other hand cannot be erased, and if you happen to make a splodge you're in trouble.'

'Won't you require a pen for your duties as regent?' Whimbrel suggested. 'Surely you'll need one for signing decrees.'

'It is not the pen that counts,' replied Smew. 'It is he who wields it.'

His words had the effect of silencing any further comment from either Whimbrel or Brambling, and after that the conversation became noticeably one-sided.

Finding myself alone I decided to go for a browse along the bookshelves, taking my glass of wine with me. Occasionally I selected a title, took down the book and read the preface. Then I put it back again and moved on. This proved to be quite a pleasant pastime. The royal collection was rich in variety: tomes on every subject stood side by side in silent ranks, all waiting to be read. After a while I came upon a book I hadn't seen since I was a child. It was called *Tales from Long Ago*, and as I lifted it down I felt a curious wave of anticipation pass through me. I remembered this book in particular because it had a colour picture on every other page, so that each story was encapsulated in a few scenes. Sure enough, when I opened it there was a page of text on the left side, and an illustration on the right. To my surprise I recognised the first picture as if I had only seen it the previous day, rather than many years before. It showed three men gazing up at the night sky through a tall, narrow window. I was astounded at the familiarity of the detail; also, the brightness of the colours. The three men wore blue coats, their shoes were buckled and their stockings were white. The words of the story, however, were unfamiliar. Slowly, I turned to the next page. Here was a man in a rowing boat in the middle of a lake; on his head was a yellow crown. I examined the picture and noticed that one of the oarlocks hadn't been drawn properly. Part of it was missing, which would have made the boat impossible to row. I recalled that this had baffled me throughout my childhood. Again, though, I had no memory of the story itself, and I began to realise that when I was young I couldn't have read the book properly. I must have spent all my time looking at the pictures. I turned the pages, one by one, and yet more half-forgotten characters were revealed. Invariably they appeared startled, bewildered, surprised or jubilant. Hidden away inside this book, they'd worn the same expressions for years and years and years. At last I arrived at the final page. I paused for a long moment. Then, as I expected, I turned over and saw a man in a broad-brimmed hat. He was peering with astonishment at a silver coin in the palm of his hand.

'Found something riveting?' said a voice behind me.

It was Wryneck.

'Not really,' I said, quickly returning the book to its place amongst the others.

Wryneck must have somehow detached himself from Sanderling. Now he'd come prowling along the bookshelves from the other direction.

'I would have thought you'd be in the music section,' he said, 'trying to keep a step ahead of your protégé.'

It took a moment to absorb the meaning of his remark.

'You mean Greylag?' I asked.

'Of course,' replied Wryneck. 'He's making extraordinary advances in the field of symphonic music. I've called in at the cake once or twice recently and the work he's doing never fails to impress me. You must be very proud of him.'

'Yes,' I said. 'I suppose I am.'

'His latest project is progressing by leaps and bounds.'

'I take it you're referring to Greylag's tonal experimentations.'

'Correct.' Wryneck was brimming with enthusiasm. 'They should provide valuable groundwork for the next composition.'

It occurred to me that I should be telling Wryneck all this, rather than him telling me; which served as a reminder that once again I'd neglected Greylag and the rest of the orchestra. Plainly, Wryneck had visited the cake more than 'once or twice' in recent days, but in any case it was more than I had.

Without a doubt he was fully aware that Greylag did all the composing, and not me, yet he was diplomatic enough to skirt around the matter. As usual I was unable to detect the precise drift of Wryneck's observations. I had no idea whether he was encouraging me to take a deeper interest in Greylag's work, or advising me not to interfere, or neither.

'Well, thank you, Wryneck,' was all I managed to say. 'Your comments are always welcome.'

Wryneck nodded, and then continued perusing the bookshelves. Meanwhile, I returned to the main party, where I discovered that most of the wine had gone. There were a few glasses remaining, however, so I helped myself. Sanderling appeared to have finished explaining the art of sailing to the others. He was now standing alone with a full glass in his hand, and a very contented look on his face. Smew was still giving Brambling and Whimbrel the benefit of his wisdom; they both seemed as if they were wilting under the strain. Dotterel and Garganey were standing somewhat aloof and talking quietly. They broke off their conversation as I approached.

'Ho ho,' I said. 'Not plotting Smew's downfall, I hope?'

'Hardly,' said Dotterel. 'A disunited cabinet is the last thing we need at a time like this.'

Something in his tone caused me to lower my voice.

'How do you mean?' I enquired.

'Isn't it obvious?' said Garganey.

'Not to me, no,' I said.

'Well,' said Dotterel, 'we're not allowed to discuss it until after the twelve-day feast. You'll just have to wait until then.'

At that moment Smew clapped his hands together and we all turned to face him. Wryneck reappeared from amongst the bookshelves.

'Thank you all for coming,' said Smew. 'I think you'll agree the afternoon has been a great success.'

There was a small ripple of applause.

'I have a parting gift for each of you,' he continued. 'If you please, Shrike.'

I'd noticed Shrike hovering in the doorway. Now he came in bearing our gifts on a tray. We were to receive a bottle of wine apiece.

'This is the fortified variety,' explained Smew, 'something to help you through the inclement weather.'

It turned out that nobody, not even Whimbrel, had thought to bring a gift for Smew, but he seemed unconcerned. He just stood there beaming. One by one we took our bottles of wine, thanked him, and made ready to leave. Sanderling was particularly fulsome in his gratitude. His eyes glistened at the thought of the twelve blissful days that lay ahead.

'We can all visit each other's departments,' he suggested, 'and share one another's wine.'

Wryneck, however, had different ideas.

'Strictly speaking, the admiralty should be closed for the duration of the feast,' he announced, 'and likewise the post office, the counting house and the ministry of works. The doors will be locked and the lights dimmed: hardly suitable for socialising.'

'No,' said Sanderling, 'I suppose not.'

'Therefore, I suggest you save your wine for remedial purposes.'

With these bleak words ringing in our ears we were ushered out into the rain, which was now bucketing down. Whimbrel waited until after the door had closed behind us.

'Don't worry, Sanderling,' he said, 'you can come up to the observatory and have a drink there.'

'You mean now?' said Sanderling.

He was clearly eager to take up the invitation.

'Well, actually I meant another day,' replied Whimbrel.

'When, though?' asked Sanderling.

'Tomorrow, perhaps,' offered Whimbrel.

'Right,' said Sanderling, 'tomorrow it is. Goodnight.'

Next moment he'd gone dashing off through the rain without arranging a proper time. Whimbrel turned to me and shrugged. Meanwhile, Dotterel, Brambling and Garganey had wandered away in separate directions, all clutching their seasonal gifts.

'I think I'll call in on the orchestra,' I said. 'See what sort of feast they've been having.'

I thought Whimbrel looked at me slightly oddly when I said this, but he passed no remark so I wished him goodnight and went on my way.

'Shall I pop round tomorrow?' I asked at the last moment.

'If you like,' Whimbrel replied.

Then he was all alone in the darkness.

★   ★   ★

So it was that the twelve-day feast began to tick slowly by. I put into immediate effect my resolve to spend more time with the orchestra. I found them, of course, just as I had left them, hard at work on Greylag's music. Obviously serfs were not granted holidays like the rest of us, so they just carried on practising as normal. Nor had they been idle during my absence. I soon discovered that Wryneck was quite correct in describing Greylag's tremendous advances. To tell the truth I'd never heard anything like it: great crashing chords greeted me as I strode down the auditorium; woodwind, brass and strings clambered over one another as they vied for my attention; themes emerged, developed and faded away, only to be resurrected once more. I felt as if I had entered some immense factory where music was being invented for the first time. Occasionally, I picked up the conductor's baton and offered my services, but most of the time Greylag remained at the helm. Whenever there was a break, which was rare, he explained what he was striving for musically; but most of it went straight over my head. From what I could gather, the nearer he got to his goal, the further it moved away. Even so, he was plainly gaining in confidence. For my part, all I could do was urge him to continue as best he could. Such was the extent of my involvement with the orchestra: they would play and I would listen.

In the world outside the feast rolled on. The Maypole, of course, served as a beacon in the surrounding winter darkness. It was always thronging with merrymakers, and more than once I was tempted to pay a return visit. My previous qualms, however, were yet to subside. Therefore, I decided to wait until after the festivities had quietened down. Instead, I spent the evenings with Whimbrel at the observatory. I was in good company. Sanderling had also become a regular fixture, and gradually the three of us worked our way through successive bottles of fortified wine. Whimbrel turned out to be a bounteous host and often provided a range of edible treats. For this reason I determined not to mention the sixpence he owed me.

My patience was tried to the limits, however, when he told us one evening how he'd spent the afternoon. Apparently he'd been to a matinée performance of Gallinule's play.

'Marvellous piece of work,' he said. 'Especially Gallinule himself as the main protagonist: what an actor!'

'Good show, was it?' asked Sanderling.

'Terrific,' replied Whimbrel. 'The tale of ambition poised before the fall.'

'I thought it was sixpence a ticket,' I ventured.

'Correct,' said Whimbrel.

'Don't you reserve your sixpence for the telescope?'

'Normally, yes,' he answered, 'but it so happened I had a spare one.'

'Really?'

'Quite by chance actually,' he continued. 'I meant to tell you about it. Two men appeared at the door yesterday morning asking if they could have a look through the telescope. I pointed out that this was the royal observatory, not a public amenity, but they were very persistent. They said they had their own coins and were prepared to reward me for any inconvenience.'

'Who were these men?' I enquired.

'No idea,' said Whimbrel. 'They had foreign accents and wore olive drab uniforms; they seemed harmless enough, though, so I took them up on to the roof.'

'Let me guess,' I said. 'They wanted to look at the railway?'

'At first, yes,' said Whimbrel, 'but then they turned to the west and spent ages peering in that direction. I told them there was nothing out there except the sea but they wouldn't listen. They just kept plying the telescope with coins as if there was no tomorrow. The pair of them certainly seemed prosperous. They each had a pocketful of money and when they left they gave me a sixpence for my trouble.'

'Did they say thank you?'

'Funny you should ask that,' said Whimbrel. 'As a matter of fact they didn't.'

'And have you still got the coin they gave you?'

'Indeed I have.'

He reached into his pocket and produced a silver sixpence; except, of course, that it wasn't a sixpence at all.

'Good grief,' said Whimbrel, 'I've been swindled.'

His face betrayed sheer astonishment as he inspected the coin properly for the first time. It was exactly the same as the one I'd been given, with a hammer and anvil on one side and CITY OF SCOFFERS on the other.

There was a long silence, and then Sanderling spoke.

'I've got one of those too,' he said, rather bashfully.

From his pocket he produced an identical coin.

'How did you come by yours?' I asked.

'I met two men in olive drab uniforms,' he said. 'They asked directions to the observatory and then gave me this.'

I decided I had better confess about my own coin as well. I told the story of how I'd acquired it, and then the three of us sat glumly pondering our foolishness.

'I've seen those men on a few occasions, around and about,' said Sanderling, 'and others like them.'

'Where?' I queried.

'All over the place, actually. They usually go in pairs and seem to be scrutinising everything.'

'You mean like tourists?'

'Not really,' said Sanderling, 'more like they're on patrol.'

'Doesn't anyone question their presence?'

Sanderling shrugged. 'It's a holiday, isn't it? Nobody pays them any attention.'

'They even came to see Gallinule's play,' said Whimbrel. 'There were two of them sitting in the back row this afternoon. Oddly enough, they appeared quite unmoved by the tragedy. There were all these characters on stage being betrayed, coerced, shamed and abandoned, not to mention simply murdered, yet the pair of them just sat there expressionless with their arms folded.'

'Maybe it wasn't their cup of tea,' suggested Sanderling.

'Yes, maybe,' agreed Whimbrel.

He picked up a wine bottle and replenished each of our glasses. The prevailing mood was sombre.

'I'd like to have seen Gallinule's play,' I remarked.

'Then why didn't you?' asked Whimbrel.

'I didn't have a sixpence,' I replied. 'Not a proper one.'

'Well, I wish you'd told me,' he said. 'I could have lent you mine.'

19

As the clock struck ten, Smew opened the register.

'Let us begin,' he said, taking up his pencil. 'Chancellor of the Exchequer?'

'Present,' said Brambling.

'Postmaster General?'

'Present,' said Garganey.

'Astronomer Royal?'

'Present,' said Whimbrel.

'Comptroller for the Admiralty?'

'Present,' said Sanderling.

'Surveyor of the Imperial Works?'

'Present,' said Dotterel.

'Pellitory-of-the-Wall?'

'Present,' said Wryneck.

'Principal Composer to the Imperial Court?'

'Present,' I said.

'Librarian-in-Chief ?'

'Present,' said Shrike.

'Good,' said Smew. 'All present and correct.'

He closed the register and set it to one side.

Shrike's swift advance through the hierarchy reminded me, once again, that I ought to begin pressing for Greylag's freedom. With all the fine work he was doing he thoroughly deserved it. This, however, was neither the time nor the place for such matters. The twelve-day feast was over and, at Dotterel's insistence, an emergency meeting of the cabinet had been convened.

'Now, Dotterel,' Smew began, 'tell us what exactly is bothering you.'

'I'm gravely concerned,' said Dotterel, 'that my artisans are being enticed away from the empire.'

'In what sense?' asked Smew.

'The railwaymen are behind it,' Dotterel continued. 'They've established recruitment pavilions at the edge of the capital and they've spent the last two weeks trying to lure my men away with promises of jobs in the east. Hundreds of skilled workers have signed up already. They're shipping them out by the trainload.'

'I see,' said Smew.

'It's not only the skilled workers,' added Garganey. 'My postmen are walking around with so-called "recruiting sixpences" jingling in their pockets. They've been accustomed to a penny a day and now they all think they're going to be living like lords.'

'Sixpence is a huge sum to a commoner,' remarked Wryneck.

'Indeed,' said Garganey, 'but actually the whole scheme's a complete fraud. The coins they've been given look identical to imperial sixpences, but were actually struck in the City of Scoffers, wherever that may be.'

'The City of Scoffers,' repeated Smew. 'The predominant society in the east.'

'You've heard of it then?'

'Of course,' Smew replied. 'It's one of the friendly cities I alluded to during my series of talks. Clearly it has expanded beyond its boundaries; and like any growing city it requires more people to work, and yet more after that.'

'So they've come here to recruit,' said Brambling.

'Correct,' said Smew.

'By fair means or foul,' intoned Garganey.

'Why foul?' Brambling enquired. 'Surely our people are signing up of their own volition: it's their choice if they want to leave the empire.'

'Not quite,' said Garganey. 'True enough, these recruitment pavilions are all above board. They're only glorified tents, actually, but rumour has it that queues of eager applicants are forming every day; once they've signed up and received their payment it's merely a question of waiting for the next available train.'

Garganey paused and glanced around the table.

'Not everyone signs up, however. Some people are recruited by roving parties whose methods are altogether different. What they do is they slip unsuspecting persons a sixpence on some pretext, for example, in return for a small favour. Once the coin has been accepted it's deemed a "consideration". Thereafter the contract is binding. That's how they snared most of my postmen.'

'Well, in my humble opinion,' said Brambling, 'anyone who accepts money from a stranger deserves all he gets. Besides which, these "recruiting sixpences" aren't legal tender. They can't spend them in the empire.'

'I was coming to that,' rejoined Garganey. 'The new coins are so ubiquitous they're beginning to circulate freely of their own accord. Even as we speak, they're being honoured in the Maypole.'

'But what about the edict,' demanded Wryneck, 'limiting sales of beers, wines and spirits?'

'I'm afraid it's fallen by the wayside,' said Garganey.

As the discussion unfolded Whimbrel, Sanderling and I remained silent. None of us looked at each other directly, but we all must have been thinking the same thing: we'd been unwittingly recruited. Vaguely I wondered what I'd let myself in for: slaving down a mine, perhaps, or going round and round on a treadmill?

I was quite surprised, then, when Sanderling raised an entirely different subject.

'This City of Scoffers,' he said. 'Do they have dancing girls?'

Before anyone could answer there was a knock on the outer door. Immediately Shrike rushed out to answer it. Then he came back.

'It was the postman,' he announced.

Smew was about to take the letter when Garganey intervened.

'In my capacity as Postmaster General I'd like to examine the postmark, if nobody minds.'

Nobody did, and Garganey quickly reached his conclusion.

'Local postage, same-day delivery,' he declared, handing the letter to Smew.

A moment later we all knew the contents. It was a final reminder from the railwaymen. They wanted their invoice settled forthwith. The letter also mentioned that we could expect a visit from Messrs Gadwall, Merganser and Grosbeak. They would meet us at the counting house at twelve o'clock.

'I suppose we have no alternative but to pay,' said Smew. 'After all, they've fulfilled their part of the bargain.' He turned to Brambling. 'Do we have enough money in the imperial purse?'

'Almost,' Brambling replied. 'We're just half-a-crown short.'

'That's the amount we lent to those strolling players,' said Wryneck. 'They'll have to pay it back immediately.'

'Well, they should have recouped the outlay by now,' remarked Dotterel. 'I gather their production has been a huge success.'

'Surely, though,' said Garganey, 'if we're down to our last half-crown we're in dire straits indeed.'

'Not necessarily,' said Smew. 'You really should have more faith in the empire. Our people are our greatest resource, and I have no doubt that together we will all pull through.'

These were precisely the kind of words I wanted to hear. Indeed, I was most impressed by Smew's bearing during this episode. He seemed to possess all the prerequisites of a true ruler of men: sound judgement, patience and calmness. Smew was unflappable, which meant that we had nothing to worry about.

'I will lead a delegation to the counting house,' he continued. 'Accompanying me will be the following officers: Chancellor of the Exchequer, Pellitory-of-the-Wall and Principal Composer to the Imperial Court. The rest of you should proceed directly to the reading room of the great library. After the meeting I intend to invite the visiting envoys for high tea; surprise them with a nice treat and demonstrate by example what the empire is capable of.'

Thus encouraged we set about getting ready for twelve o'clock. Exactly why Smew had chosen me to join the delegation I had no idea, but I was determined to live up to the part. Accordingly, I decided to wear my dandy coat, which I happened to have left at the cake. There was just time to retrieve it before the scheduled meeting, so with Smew's permission I hurried off.

When I reached the cake I found Greylag in a very ruffled state. His usual manner was placid to say the least, but when I entered the auditorium he had a hunted look about him. The orchestra were all sitting fiddling with their instruments distractedly, while Greylag paced around in front of them.

'Greylag,' I said. 'Whatever is the matter?'

It took a few moments for Greylag to recover, and then I sat him down and got him to tell me all about it.

'I'm sorry, sir,' he said, 'but these two men were here not half an hour ago. They asked all sorts of questions about the orchestra: how many musicians do we have; how many pieces in our repertoire; how many instruments in each section; how many years' experience as musicians; they even went through my manuscripts.'

'Did they leave them all intact?' I enquired.

'Yes,' said Greylag. 'They handled everything very carefully, but they shouldn't have interrupted our work, should they, sir? We're supposed to be getting on and they made us stop.'

The visitation had clearly affected him, but I concluded that no real harm had been done apart from the break in his creative process. I felt sympathetic nevertheless. After all, he was quite unused to having outsiders poking around when he was carrying out his duties.

'I don't suppose these men were dressed in olive drab, were they?' I asked, although I already knew the answer.

'Yes, they were, sir,' said Greylag, 'both of them.'

'Did they give you anything?'

'No, sir.'

'Well, never mind,' I said. 'They've gone now.'

'But they shouldn't have been here, should they, sir?'

'No,' I concurred, 'not without asking.'

I couldn't afford to delay any longer, so I assured Greylag he wouldn't be disturbed again, then collected my dandy coat and headed back. The delegation was just about to leave when I arrived. Smew was now wearing the ceremonial crown. Wryneck and Brambling were both attired in their smartest outfits. I joined them and we set off for the counting house. It wasn't quite twelve yet, but the three men were already waiting at the door. As I expected, they were all dressed in olive drab uniforms. I recognised Gadwall from our previous encounters. His official title was Commissioner of Railways for the City of Scoffers. Merganser turned out to be the man who'd tipped me my silver 'sixpence'. He was introduced as Chief Recruiting Agent for the City of Scoffers. The third man I hadn't seen before. His name was Grosbeak, and he announced himself as City Treasurer. Apparently he didn't consider it necessary to mention which city he was referring to; and this omission more or less set the tone for the proceedings. Several times during the ensuing talks the three men referred simply to 'the city' as if we were already quite familiar with its every detail. Furthermore, they made it clear that they regarded the empire as little more than peripheral to the City of Scoffers, which in turn they seemed to think was at the centre of the universe. They spoke as though it had been extant for a thousand years, rather than a few fortuitous decades; and when compared with the City of Scoffers all else paled into insignificance.

Centre of the universe or not, it was certainly the centre of an integrated railway system. We quickly gathered that the network radiated in all directions from a vast industrial heartland. Just lately a new spoke had been extended into Greater Fallowfields; and now the contractors were demanding payment. It transpired that Grosbeak handled the collection of debt.

Before discussing terms, however, Smew insisted that the correct protocol be followed. He began, therefore, by presenting his officers-of-state. First to step forward was Wryneck, who managed to give a very good account of himself. He had obviously done his homework and knew just enough about railway gauges to hold his own in polite conversation. He bowed curtly to Grosbeak, and the gesture was duly returned.

When my turn came, Smew accidentally introduced me as Principal Conductor to the Imperial Court.

'Principal Composer, actually,' I said, shaking hands with Grosbeak, 'although I do conduct from time to time. I'm in charge of the imperial orchestra.'

Grosbeak raised his eyebrows.

'Ah, yes,' he said, 'the philharmonic host.'

This phrase struck me as being rather dismissive, and my initial assumption was that Grosbeak had no interest whatsoever in music. Yet plainly he was aware of the orchestra's existence. Then I remembered Greylag's report about the two men who'd turned up at the cake asking all sorts of questions. It sounded to me as if they were 'taking stock' of the orchestra, preparing an inventory so to speak, and vaguely I wondered if Grosbeak had anything to do with it.

Meanwhile, the spotlight had turned on Brambling.

'Financial matters are dealt with here at the counting house,' declared Smew, 'so if you have no objection I'll leave you in Brambling's care; and hope to see you afterwards for tea?'

Evidently Smew believed he had done all he needed to do. He gave each of us a courteous nod, then strode off in the direction of the great library. Wryneck went with him, but I decided to stay and provide Brambling with some moral support. His chosen approach was seemingly one of openness.

'Well, gentlemen,' he began, 'we've received your invoice and we're prepared to offer an immediate deposit.'

'Indeed?' said Grosbeak.

'The balance to be settled within seven days,' Brambling added.

Grosbeak conferred briefly with Gadwall and Merganser before replying.

'This is not our normal way of doing business,' he said. 'Seven days is a long while to withhold such a large sum, especially when you've had twelve days already.' He paused. 'However, it so happens we have further matters to address which could arguably take another week. In consequence we agree to accept your deposit. I presume it's cash?'

'Yes it is,' replied Brambling, 'so if you'd just care to step inside?'

We filed into the counting house and Brambling led us to the iron-bound treasure chest.

'Here we are,' he said.

He then made a bit of a performance out of finding the key, which he pretended to have lost on his person. I guessed that the idea of this jape was to lighten the general mood, but it failed to raise even a smile from the three creditors. Instead, they merely stood watching his antics with sober expressions on their faces. Finally he located the key and unlocked the chest.

The hoard of sixpences, shillings and half-crowns certainly looked impressive as it gleamed in the fading afternoon light. I was therefore surprised by the collective reaction of Grosbeak, Gadwall and Merganser. The sound they uttered, apparently in unison, was difficult to describe. It was part guffaw, part smirk and part sneer; and was so unexpected that Brambling and I glanced at one another warily. Without invitation Grosbeak scooped up a handful of coins, examined them momentarily, and allowed them to trickle between his fingers.

Then he turned to Brambling.

'We can't accept this,' he said.

'Why not?' asked Brambling.

'It's worthless.'

'How can it be worthless?' protested Brambling. 'This is the imperial currency!'

Grosbeak raised his hand.

'I should correct myself,' he said. 'This money is no longer recognised as international exchange.'

'Since when?'

'For at least a decade.'

'So we can't use it to settle the debt?'

'I'm afraid not,' said Grosbeak. 'There is only one valid means of payment nowadays.'

He dipped into his pocket and produced a coin, which he held flat in the palm of his hand. It was identical to the 'sixpence' I'd received from Merganser.

'We call this the anvil,' Grosbeak announced, 'although its proper designation is the "currency unit of the City of Scoffers".'

'Also known as CoS,' I ventured.

'Quite so,' said Grosbeak.

There was a brief hiatus as Brambling sank on to a chair. He was clearly shaken by this unheralded turn of events and needed to catch his breath.

In the meantime, Merganser went over to the table and peered down at Brambling's ledger. Then, slowly and deliberately, he began turning the pages. He was soon joined by Grosbeak, and the two of them spent several minutes scrutinising the contents.

'Is this a full record of the empire's financial affairs?' asked Grosbeak.

'Yes,' Brambling replied, 'it's all there in the finest detail.'

'Then you won't mind if we borrow it to see if we can find a way out of this impasse?'

'I suppose not.'

'Very well,' said Grosbeak, closing the ledger again. 'I'll send my men to collect it later.'

Brambling nodded despondently.

'Right,' I said in my brightest tone, 'now that's settled we can all go and have some tea.'

I bustled around and tried to make light of the entire matter, as though we officers-of-state were accustomed to dealing with such crises. Seizing Grosbeak by the arm I led him out into the open air; we were followed by Gadwall and

Merganser, and quickly we set off towards the great library. Brambling came trailing along behind.

When we entered the reading room we discovered that elaborate preparations had been made to ensure this 'tea party' was a success. It was too late in the season to furnish a spectacular sunset through the bay window. Nonetheless, the room looked quite resplendent. The chandeliers had been lit, the imperial flag hung from the ceiling, and the walls were decorated with garlands. Smew had dispensed with the ceremonial crown and was now wearing his lounge suit, presumably to make the guests feel more at home. Dotterel, Garganey and Whimbrel were standing around in relaxed poses, while Sanderling helped Shrike serve the tea and toasted soldiers.

Smew was geniality itself.

'Everything satisfactory?' he asked, when we'd all assembled around him.

'More or less,' Grosbeak replied.

'Then I must show you around the library.'

There had been no real opportunity to explain the situation to Smew, but when I thought about it I realised it wasn't particularly urgent. After all, he was under the impression that in the past half hour the imperial reserves had been reduced to nothing. The fact that they'd been rejected as worthless was hardly better news. For this reason it was probably wiser to let him carry on playing the host uninterrupted. He would doubtless learn the truth later.

His intimate knowledge of the library was now coming to the fore. He obviously delighted in showing the three visitors around, occasionally lifting down odd volumes for them to look at more closely, and generally acclaiming the quality of the vast collection.

'Who owns all these books?' enquired Merganser at one point. 'The citizens of Greater Fallowfields?'

'No,' Smew answered, 'they belong to the emperor.'

Grosbeak raised his eyebrows.

'Ah, yes,' he said, 'the imperial truant.'

'Truant?' repeated Smew, visibly startled. 'How so?'

'Your esteemed emperor enrolled at our university last term,' said Merganser. 'He ceased attending lectures after only a few weeks and we haven't seen him since.'

'Did you try his board and lodgings?'

'Naturally,' said Grosbeak. 'It seems he left without paying the rent.'

With this stunning revelation ringing in our ears we resumed our tour of the library. Ostensibly the empire was disintegrating beneath our very feet, yet all we could do was wander along the shelves looking at books. In due course we arrived back in the reading room, where more tea was waiting to be served. By now Smew appeared to have gathered his thoughts.

'This contract for the railway,' he said. 'When did the emperor sign it?'

'During the first week of term,' replied Grosbeak.

'I see.' Smew frowned. 'Well, I can only apologise for His Majesty's continued absence. I dare say there's a perfectly simple explanation.'

'Possibly,' conceded Grosbeak.

'In the meantime,' Smew continued, 'I very much hope the three of you aren't planning on leaving us just yet?'

'We intend to stay for at least another week,' said Grosbeak.

'Good,' said Smew. 'Now is there anything else I can do for you?'

Grosbeak thought for a moment.

'Yes,' he said, 'we would like to sample your cake.'

20

A special concert was organised for the following evening, the guests of honour being Grosbeak, Merganser and Gadwall. It was all rather hastily arranged, and I suspected that Smew was trying to appease them. By now, of course, he'd been informed of the outstanding debt. He was clearly hoping to buy time, so it was imperative that I gave him my full backing. I went to see Greylag as soon as I learned of the plan, and told him we'd expect an exceptional performance. Quickly we agreed that the best policy was for the orchestra to play some variations on the imperial anthem, followed by Greylag's recent overture.

'Nothing experimental,' I urged. 'Not for these people.'

'As you wish, sir,' said Greylag, though it was evident he was disappointed. He had plainly moved on from 'mere' anthems and overtures.

Rehearsals would be held during the afternoon, with the concert beginning at seven o'clock sharp. I helped out where I could; and while I was checking the seating schedule I happened to glance down at the orchestra. Once again I couldn't help noticing the threadbare nature of their frock coats. We were supposed to be trying to impress the deputation from the City of Scoffers, yet the imperial orchestra was dressed in worn-out clothes! I decided that something must be done about it, and after some thought I headed over to the ministry of works. Maybe Dotterel would have a supply of spare outfits stored in some warehouse or other.

To my surprise, I found him sitting in his office deep in conversation with Garganey. They didn't take kindly to being interrupted.

'Yes,' said Dotterel, 'what is it?'

'Sorry to bother you,' I said, 'but I was wondering if you had any frock coats in the imperial livery?'

'Why should I have?'

'I just thought you might, that's all.'

Dotterel looked at Garganey and slowly shook his head. Then he addressed me again.

'You want them for the orchestra, I suppose?'

'Correct,' I said.

'Well, the answer is no,' said Dotterel. 'The orchestra is your responsibility, not mine; and to be quite frank you should have provided them with new coats long ago.'

'Me?' I retorted. 'How could I provide them?'

'You receive a stipend, don't you?'

'Yes.'

'Then you have your solution,' proclaimed Dotterel. 'Go to a draper's shop and buy some.'

I puffed out my cheeks.

'Oh,' I said, 'right.'

During the conversation Garganey had remained silent. Now I turned to him.

'Just out of interest,' I said, 'where do the postmen get their uniforms?'

'They're supplied by the post office,' he answered.

I thanked them both for their time and bid them good-day.

'Don't forget tonight's concert,' I said as I departed.

'No,' said Dotterel, 'we won't.'

I hurried back to the cake. Obviously I wouldn't be able to acquire any new clothes before the performance, but I made a mental note to tackle the problem as soon as possible afterwards. Meanwhile, the lights over the orchestra pit would have to be kept dim.

The hours were marching quickly by, and soon it was six thirty. I spoke to Greylag and he assured me that the orchestra was fully prepared.

'Excellent,' I said. 'Well, good luck, Greylag, and I'll see you later on.'

The musicians were giving their instruments a final inspection; I left them to it and took up my position at the front door. A full house was expected, word having spread about the interest expressed by the visitors. Punctual as ever, Grosbeak, Merganser and Gadwall arrived at ten to seven, wearing appropriate dress uniform. This comprised the usual olive drab, but with the addition of creamy-white ornamental braiding. The imperial officers-of-state all turned up in good time, attired in their finest dandy coats. They were followed by select members of the public, assorted postmen and artisans and then, finally, the troupe of strolling players. Gallinule led the latter inside with his usual flourish. I noticed once again that Mestolone was absent from their company. This was the second occasion to my knowledge that he'd steered clear of the newcomers, and I began to surmise that he wasn't particularly keen on them. Still, there was no time to dwell further on the matter. It was a minute to seven so I made my way to my seat.

I'd taken care to reserve a place where I could keep an eye on our three distinguished guests. I was especially interested to see how they would react to the performance; Whimbrel's account of Gallinule's play was still fresh in my mind. According to Whimbrel, two of these men in olive drab had watched the entire tragedy with apparent detachment. As Greylag stepped on to the podium, I pondered whether his wonderful music would get through to Grosbeak, Merganser and Gadwall.

We were to begin with the fifth, sixth and seventh variations on the imperial anthem. I considered these to be the most stirring of Greylag's treatments and had requested them specifically. With ninety-eight musicians at his disposal we could certainly expect some fireworks from Greylag.

The response of the audience in general was most encouraging. The moment Greylag raised his baton a great hush descended. Then they sat mesmerised as the orchestra got into its stride. The standard, as ever, was first class. After a few minutes I looked sidelong at the three 'scoffers'. Sure enough, they were all sitting expressionless with their arms folded.

Perhaps, I concluded, the imperial anthem meant nothing to them. Admittedly, they joined in the applause when the three variations were finished, but all the same I hoped they would show a little more enthusiasm for Greylag's overture, which was due to follow.

Another member of the audience was Hobby the confectioner. He was sitting fairly near to Grosbeak, Merganser and Gadwall, and was clearly enjoying himself. He hurrahed loudly at the end of each piece of music, and when the overture began he could be heard tapping his foot. Unfortunately, he had the habit of coughing during quiet passages. Not only that, but he made no attempt to do it discreetly: instead he seemed to make a performance out of each cough, producing a handkerchief and disgorging himself with gusto. It was during one such bout of coughing that I noticed Grosbeak looking across at Hobby. Next moment he gave a signal and three men in olive drab uniforms emerged from the shadows. They approached Hobby and spoke to him in lowered voices before leading him outside. He didn't come back; and subsequently there was no more coughing in the auditorium.

The overture had now reached its famous crescendo. A cheer rose up when the lone horn appeared and played its mournful notes. Then the entire orchestra came crashing back and the music charged to its tremendous finale. The concert was undoubtedly a triumph: the audience responded tumultuously. Even Grosbeak, Merganser and Gadwall were seemingly engaged at last, nodding to one another as they added to the applause. I looked over to Smew: he was smiling with evident satisfaction.

Greylag, in the meantime, had silently rejoined the orchestra as they packed away their instruments. I intended to rush over and congratulate him but no sooner had I got to my feet than I was engulfed by a crowd of well-wishers, all slapping me on the back for my supposed *tour de force*. Then Smew called me across to join his entourage. He went sweeping out into the night and I had no option but to follow; which meant that Greylag would have to wait until the following day.

By then, however, events had begun to unfold rather swiftly. It was quite a while before I had the chance to speak to Greylag again.

I was on my way to the cake next morning when I learned some disturbing news: Brambling had been so upset by the failure of the currency that he'd resigned his post as Chancellor. The first I knew of it was when I saw him standing outside the counting house with his bags packed. Apparently, he'd already seen Smew and had his resignation accepted.

'Didn't he try and persuade you to reconsider?' I asked.

'Oh yes,' replied Brambling, 'he offered the usual platitudes but I'm afraid it was too little too late. I've made up my mind to go and I'm not changing it again.'

'What are you planning to do?'

'I intend to return to the provinces and fade into obscurity.'

Nevertheless, his duties were incomplete. He wasn't going anywhere until he'd seen the ledger returned safely to its rightful home.

'Those scrutineers won't find any errors,' he declared, 'if that's what they're looking for.'

I felt slightly sorry for Brambling. After all, it wasn't his fault that the currency was worthless; indeed, the slide had begun years before he commenced his brief tenure. Everyone always assumed that Greater Fallowfields possessed vast reserves of gold and silver bullion, but now the assumption was shown to be untrue. All we had was a hoard of coins whose value depended on the good name of the empire. This, it transpired, was no longer enough: the empire was on the wane. We couldn't even resort to buried treasure. Hidden somewhere was a crown of solid gold, but nobody knew where it was. Consequently we were unable to pay our debts, and Brambling blamed himself. I left him brooding and continued my journey towards the cake.

When I arrived I was confronted by a huge number of parcels stacked outside the main door. There were roughly a hundred of them, all wrapped in brown paper, and I guessed they were the orchestra's new coats. This was typical of the empire: necessary items could never be found until *after* they were needed. I decided that Dotterel must have had a change of heart; presumably he'd located the garments and ordered these parcels to be dispatched forthwith, but the postmen had then failed to deliver them in time for the concert.

On examining the parcels closely, however, I discovered that they did not bear the imperial postmark. Instead, they were all stamped with the letters CoS.

Quickly I opened one of them. Inside, neatly pressed and folded, was an olive drab uniform. I was still standing there holding it when Whimbrel appeared.

'We're wanted down at the counting house,' he said, 'urgently.'

I rewrapped the parcel and put it back on its pile. Then we set off. As we walked, I informed Whimbrel about Brambling's impending departure. He was unsurprised.

'Dotterel and Garganey have tendered their resignations too,' he said. 'It seems they've had the idea of combining the workforce into some kind of trade organisation before it dwindles any further. They've both come to the conclusion that workers can't be ruled from the top down; so they've decided to join their ranks and develop a democratic movement.'

'Is that why we're needed at the counting house?' I enquired.

'No,' replied Whimbrel, 'but the matter is equally serious. Grosbeak and his men have returned with the ledger.'

There was a small gathering outside the counting house when we got there. Smew was present, of course, as well as Wryneck and Shrike. Representing the visitors were Grosbeak and Merganser, accompanied by a few of their henchmen; but we saw no sign of Brambling.

'He's gone,' explained Wryneck. 'He headed off as soon as the ledger was safely returned.'

'Didn't he say goodbye?' I asked.

'He did to me, yes,' said Wryneck.

'And me,' added Shrike.

'Well, he didn't to me,' I said.

'Can we please get on?' demanded Grosbeak.

'Certainly,' said Smew. 'Let's go inside.'

One of Grosbeak's assistants had laid the ledger on the table, and now we assembled around it. Grosbeak settled down in Brambling's former chair. Smew sat opposite. As *de facto* regent he was our natural spokesman.

'We have studied your records,' Grosbeak began, 'and they are reasonably transparent.'

'Good,' said Smew.

'You have a negative balance of half-a-crown.'

'So I believe.'

Grosbeak opened the ledger at a certain page.

'Let's get straight down to business,' he continued. 'We are prepared to defer the cash payment as long as three conditions are fulfilled.'

'Just a moment,' murmured Smew. He reached into his pocket and produced his notepad and pencil. Then he sat holding them at the ready. 'Well,' he said, 'what are these conditions?'

'Firstly, that the empire adopts Standard Railway Time.'

'Ah,' said Smew, 'the march of progress.'

'It's quite elemental,' Grosbeak commented. 'You need to be integrated into the network and you might as well do it now as later.'

'We've recently put a lot of effort into setting our clocks for winter,' said Whimbrel.

'That can't be helped,' said Grosbeak. 'You'll just have to reset them.'

'Let's hear the second condition,' said Smew.

'We wish to requisition your cake. It is a fine building with a large capacity: we propose to use it for future recruitment rallies.'

'What about the orchestra?' I objected. 'They have nowhere else to go.'

'I was coming to that,' said Grosbeak. He referred briefly to the ledger. 'I understand that the imperial orchestra consists entirely of serfs.'

'Correct,' said Smew.

'These serfs being the property of the crown estates: actually the only portable property.'

As Grosbeak uttered these words I sensed Whimbrel stirring beside me. I began to feel rather uneasy, and even Wryneck drew a deep breath.

'Such is the nature of serfdom, yes,' said Smew warily.

'Then the third condition is that the orchestra be taken into our protection and removed to the City of Scoffers.'

'That's not fair,' said Wryneck.

'Fairness doesn't enter into it,' replied Grosbeak. 'Those are our terms. Don't forget, we're the injured party, not you. We built the railway as per the contract. Now we desire recompense. It's as simple as that.'

'Yes, yes,' said Smew, 'we fully understand.'

At that instant a shrill whistle was heard in the distance.

Grosbeak looked at his watch.

'Five o'clock,' he announced. 'The evening train is exactly on schedule.'

Simultaneously, public clocks all around the capital began to strike eleven. Or some of them did anyway. Others played a short melody and *then* chimed the hour. As I listened it quickly became evident that a few of these clocks needed urgent attention. They'd only been adjusted about two weeks previously, yet half of them sounded as if they'd lost several minutes already! No sooner would one clock complete its cycle of chimes than another would start up nearby, then another after that, as though they were arguing about precisely what time it was. Of course, as far as Grosbeak was concerned they were all 'wrong'. If his first condition was to be met, then someone would have to go around altering them again. Without Dotterel on hand to oversee the task, I wondered how this could possibly be achieved.

Equally unsettling was Grosbeak's second condition. It appeared that the 'recruitment pavilions' near the railway were no longer sufficient for his requirements. Instead, he wanted to take over the cake and hold mass rallies there. How the populace would view such a prospect was anybody's guess: we simply didn't do that kind of thing in the empire, and especially not in the capital.

It was the third condition, however, that was most disturbing of all. Grosbeak intended to transplant the orchestra to the City of Scoffers, which meant, effectively, that I'd be out of a job. Oh, I was fully aware that my role as Principal Composer was merely nominal. Everyone knew who the real composer was. Nonetheless, as an officer-of-state I still felt that I had much to contribute. To be quite truthful I enjoyed being a

member of the cabinet, not only for the privileges it conferred, but also because it put me at the very heart of imperial
affairs. With the orchestra gone, my position would be far less
tenable.

While I was pondering all this, Smew had been busily in
consultation with Wryneck. The two of them stood slightly
apart from the rest of us with their heads together, talking
quietly.

Now Smew turned to Grosbeak. 'We feel that you leave
us little choice,' he said. 'The honour of the empire must be
preserved and therefore we agree to your conditions.'

'Excellent,' Grosbeak replied. 'We will begin operations
tomorrow.'

Whimbrel was in a sombre mood when I visited him at the
observatory that evening. He said nothing when he let me in,
and remained silent as we climbed the iron stairway. Then we
sat at his table and drank the remaining drops of our fortified
wine. I'd called in at the cake on my way over and broken
the news to Greylag. He'd accepted it in his normal resigned
manner, a fact which came as a relief to me. The last thing
I needed was Greylag kicking up a fuss. Apparently, some
of Grosbeak's men had paid a visit during the afternoon and
distributed the new outfits. Each musician now sat with an
unopened brown-paper parcel at his feet. Rehearsals had been
discontinued and all the instrument cases were packed in pre-
paredness for their departure. They'd been told to be ready to
leave by ten o'clock the following morning (local time).

'A final concession to the empire,' remarked Whimbrel. 'Henceforward, we'll all be living in Standard Railway Time.'

We peered through the observatory window. In the moonlight we could see a large flag fluttering above the cake, emblazoned with a hammer and anvil. Similar flags had also been hoisted at various locations across the capital, the flags of the empire having first been lowered.

'They're very self-assured, aren't they?' I said. 'Confident to the point of arrogance, actually.'

'Maybe so,' said Whimbrel, 'but there's something bothering them all the same.'

'How do you mean?' I asked.

'I've lost count of the number of times they've come here demanding to look through the telescope. True, they always bring a pocketful of sixpences, or anvils as they prefer to call them: they never fail to pay their way. Yet they always turn the telescope to the west and spend hours gazing towards the sea. I've told them repeatedly that there's nothing out there but they won't listen. They just continue pouring coins into the slot.'

'What do you think they're watching for?'

'I don't know,' said Whimbrel. 'It's almost as if they're on guard against some hidden menace lurking just beyond the horizon.'

'Well, at least the empire's recouping some money,' I said. 'We need every penny we can get.'

After that the conversation subsided into silence again. We

each sat with our own thoughts as the sky darkened and the stars appeared over the occupied capital.

By next morning I'd decided that I really ought to try and do something for the orchestra. Remembering my failed attempt to buy them all some sweets, I determined to tackle the confectioner once again. Maybe he would accept my 'recruiting sixpence' as payment, especially now that the coins were circulating throughout the realm. When I arrived at the sweetshop, however, I found the door locked and a sign hanging outside: CLOSED UNTIL FURTHER NOTICE. I looked through the window at all the sweets in their jars, as inviting and unreachable as ever. Then I turned and headed for the railway station.

Much had changed since my previous visit: apart from the main line there was now a siding with a loop in the track so that trains could be turned around without uncoupling; a prefabricated building labelled PROCESSING CENTRE had replaced the former encampment; and the station platform had been provided with wooden benches.

A train was waiting with all its carriage doors open. Sitting on a bench was Whimbrel, who I'd arranged to meet at ten o'clock so that we could say goodbye to the orchestra.

'I hope they're going to be all right,' he said. 'They've never travelled anywhere before, as far as I know.'

His concern for the orchestra was quite touching. After all, they were my responsibility, not his. Even so, I didn't really think there was much to worry about. Grosbeak and his companions may have driven a hard bargain, but I sensed that they meant no harm to the orchestra: according to the agreement the musicians were being taken into 'protection'. This sounded innocuous enough to me, though Wryneck had raised a voice of protest when it was first proposed. Also, I vaguely recalled Mestolone mentioning something about 'protection' some weeks earlier.

As a matter of fact, Whimbrel had some fresh tidings and they concerned Mestolone. Apparently, he had offered his services to help with the adjustment and maintenance of the public clocks. He'd approached Smew and explained that he wished to assist the empire in its hour of need; and whilst he had no desire to collaborate with the 'scoffers', he realised it was necessary at least to be seen co-operating.

'Did Smew accept the offer?' I asked.

'Without hesitation,' Whimbrel rejoined. 'Actually he's made Mestolone an honorary citizen of Greater Fallowfields.'

'What about the other actors?'

'It seems they've been keeping a low profile,' said Whimbrel. 'They're ensconced in the Maypole and living on credit.'

'Just for a change,' I remarked.

A nearby clock began striking ten, and a file of men came marching along the platform. It took me a moment to recognise them as members of the orchestra, because they were all now wearing their new olive drab uniforms. They carried with them their instrument cases but appeared to have few other possessions. Last to arrive was Greylag. When he saw me and Whimbrel he paused.

'Morning, Greylag,' I said. 'All set?'

'Yes, sir,' he replied.

'Looks as if you've got a long journey ahead of you.'

'Yes.'

The orchestra was accompanied by several of Grosbeak's henchmen. I thought they spoke rather gruffly as they ordered the musicians into the carriages, but I assumed they had a strict timetable to adhere to. For this reason their impatience could be excused.

'Well, good luck, Greylag,' I ventured, shaking his hand.

'Thank you, sir,' he said.

Likewise, Whimbrel shook hands with Greylag; he also slipped a silver coin into his pocket.

'You may find it useful,' he said.

Greylag thanked him, then turned and climbed into his allotted carriage. He didn't give me a second glance. Further along the platform a whistle was blown; immediately the engine blew its own whistle in response. Whimbrel and I stepped back a little as the wheels began to turn.

'I've been hoping to secure Greylag's freedom,' I said, 'but it's too late now.'

'Yes,' Whimbrel agreed, 'it's too late now.'

Greylag was lost from view. We watched as the train rolled slowly out of the station, carrying him off to the City of Scoffers.

21

'Might just make it!' cried a blur that came hurtling past us.

It was Sanderling. He was running as fast as his legs would carry him, clutching a valise in one hand and a railway ticket in the other. His dandy coat was all unbuttoned, so that it flapped wildly around him as he rushed along. Some of the train's sliding doors remained open, and Sanderling clearly thought he had a chance of catching it. Unfortunately, such was his haste that his hat came off his head and he failed even to notice. It went bowling along the platform behind him; quickly I dashed after it, picked it up and set off in pursuit. By now he had drawn level with the last carriage and managed to swing his bag through the doorway. At the same instant a pair of hands grabbed him by the shoulders and helped him inside. Summoning a final spurt, I caught up with the train and tossed his hat into the carriage. Then a second pair of hands grabbed me and pulled me aboard, so that I landed in a heap next to Sanderling. I looked up and saw Gadwall gazing down at me.

'Glad you decided to join us,' he said.

The train was now gathering speed. I took a few seconds to get my breath back, then went to the door and peered out. In the distance I could see the diminishing figure of Whimbrel, still standing on the platform.

'I suppose the train can't be stopped?' I enquired.

'Correct,' answered Gadwall. He leant over and slid the door closed. 'Better safe than sorry,' he added.

Sanderling looked at me and shrugged.

'Apologies for that,' he said. 'Thanks for saving my hat though.'

'Don't mention it,' I replied.

There were about twenty of us in the carriage, including Greylag and perhaps fifteen other musicians. The interior was bare, with no seats apart from a folding one at the far end. This had already been taken by one of the 'guards', so the rest of us made ourselves as comfortable as we could along the rough wooden walls. After a while Gadwall came and sat down beside me and Sanderling.

The train rattled on towards the east.

We'd been sitting there for thirty minutes when Sanderling broke the silence.

'Why aren't there any windows?' he asked.

'Nothing to see,' said Gadwall.

'I notice there aren't any lights either,' Sanderling continued, 'only those ventilation slits. What happens when it gets dark?'

'We can all go to sleep.'

Gadwall's blunt rejoinder more or less put paid to any further discussion. He was far from unfriendly, however, and in due course he took a bar of chocolate from his pocket. This he passed around the carriage, inviting everyone to partake. When it ran out, one of his companions produced a similar bar. This, too, was shared amongst all and sundry, including the members of the orchestra. Evidently some of them had never tasted chocolate before, and the perceived act of kindness was enough to create a friendly atmosphere for the next few hours.

At some stage I must have drifted off to sleep. When I awoke night had fallen and I realised the train had come to a halt. Inside the carriage all was quiet, but I could hear faint voices outside; also some occasional footsteps. Light dappled momentarily through the ventilation slit, as if a lamp was being swung in the darkness. A minute passed and then there was a loud *clunk* and the train juddered: presumably some additional carriages were being attached. The sudden movement roused Sanderling briefly. He opened his eyes, rubbed them and asked where we were. When I told him I didn't know he grunted and went straight back to sleep. There were some more voices nearby; then the lamplight gradually receded. After another delay a whistle was blown and the train began moving again, quite slowly. We trundled along at a steady pace for what felt like an hour before gathering speed once more. I had no idea how many miles we'd travelled, or how many more there were to go. I just sat there staring up at a narrow strip of fathomless sky until eventually I, too, went back to sleep.

When next I surfaced I heard a bell clanging and a voice crying out 'City of Scoffers!' It was rather cold. The pale light of dawn crept into the carriage as we emerged, one by one, from our slumbers. Somebody opened the sliding door from the outside; Sanderling was fully awake in an instant.

'Ah good,' he said, standing up and fastening his dandy coat. 'We're here.'

The train had drawn into a large station with at least a dozen platforms. There was frantic activity everywhere: carriages being loaded and unloaded, and passengers disembarking. Another train was waiting at the far side of our own platform: it was facing in the opposite direction and obviously preparing to leave. This was a most welcome sight. It meant I simply had to cross over, hop aboard and I'd soon be on my way back to Fallowfields.

First, though, I considered it only proper to bid farewell to my travelling companions. Greylag and the rest of the orchestra were already being 'rounded up' by some of Gadwall's assistants. They got down from the train and assembled in a large group while a headcount was carried out. I was about to go and speak to Greylag when I spotted Sanderling stalking off down the platform.

'Sanderling!' I called, but he didn't seem to hear. 'Sanderling!' I repeated.

He had a very single-minded look about him, and I thought I had a good idea what he was going in search of. I made an attempt to follow, but he was moving through the crowd so rapidly that I soon lost sight of him. By now the orchestra had formed into two files and was beginning to march away. Greylag was in the lead.

'Goodbye, Greylag!' I called, as he passed me by, but he didn't hear me either.

Gadwall himself had hurried off the minute the carriage door opened, which meant I was now alone. With everybody gone about their business, I decided I might as well take my leave at once.

When I tried to board the other train, however, a uniformed man appeared and asked me for my ticket. When I told him I hadn't got one he politely directed me to the ticket hall. There were a number of small windows with men sitting behind them. I chose one at random and spoke through the opening.

'A ticket for Fallowfields, please.'

I placed my solitary anvil on the counter.

'Travel permit?' said the booking clerk.

'I haven't got one,' I replied.

'Outbound journeys require a travel permit.'

'Where do I get one of those?'

'Passes and permits.'

He pointed towards the far end of the hall. I thanked him and he smiled politely before closing his window and turning away. I glanced across towards my train: doors were being closed and whistles were being blown.

'Damn!' I thought to myself. 'I'm going to miss it!'

All the same, I realised I had no alternative but to go and find out about a travel permit. Doubtless another train would be leaving in an hour or so, so I retrieved my coin and wandered along the ticket hall. Now that I had a little more time on my hands I was able to take in my surroundings properly. On first impressions it was all extremely well organised. The vast interior had countless windows, timetables and notices displaying departures and arrivals; there was also a left luggage office, a lost property office, a parcels dispatch office, a waiting room and a booth selling platform tickets. In a far corner I found the department I was seeking: PASSES AND PERMITS. I approached the window and rang a bell.

Presently a man appeared. 'Can I help?'

'Yes,' I said. 'I need a travel permit, please.'

'Right you are.'

He looked down at the counter as if expecting to see something lying there. I produced my anvil and placed it before him.

'No, no,' he said, 'I have to check your reference; from your employer. What's your job?'

'I haven't got a job.'

'Haven't got a job?' he repeated. 'How can you not have a job in the City of Scoffers?'

He said this in such an incredulous tone that two or three of his colleagues joined him at the window and peered out at me with curiosity.

'I've only just got here,' I explained.

His colleague on the right said something to him quietly; then he leaned forward and looked me up and down. I was wearing my dandy coat but I had no luggage with me because of my surprise departure. After appraising me for several moments he spoke at last.

'A Fallowfieldsman, I presume?'

'Correct,' I said.

'Well,' he declared, 'we can't make any exceptions, not even for you people.'

I wasn't sure what he meant by this.

'What should I do then?' I asked.

Fortunately, his associates had started to lose interest in me and were drifting away. Otherwise they'd have witnessed my obvious shock when he gave his reply.

'You'll have to get a job,' he said. 'There's an employment exchange at the corner of the street.'

Reeling from this piece of information I retraced my steps down the length of the ticket hall, arriving at the platform just in time to see my train departing. I walked slowly after it as it clanked and swayed over the points and into the wasteland beyond the city. When I reached the end of the platform I stopped. I could hardly believe what had happened. Gradually the retreating train dwindled until it could be seen or heard no more, yet still I remained standing where I was. For ages and ages I stared blankly across the railway tracks, scarcely aware of the desultory gusts of wind that tugged at my coat, or the restless engines shunting back and forth along the sidings. Behind the station loomed tall buildings shrouded in vapour; factory hooters were blaring and smoke was rising from their immense chimneys; sparks flew inside cavernous steel sheds; beneath a gantry an iron girder descended steadily on a hook and chain; cables unwound from revolving drums; all around me the City of Scoffers was gathering momentum for the day ahead, while I could do nothing but gaze haplessly into an apparent void.

It was only when my stomach started rumbling that I remembered I hadn't eaten for several hours. With new determination I turned around and headed for the front entrance of the station. After a hearty breakfast, I resolved, everything would begin to look a lot better.

When I got out into the street there were crowds surging in all directions, but I managed to get my bearings and went in search of some sustenance. By peeking through a few windows I soon discovered that two kinds of establishment served breakfast: there were canteens which charged one anvil, and restaurants which charged two. From what I could gather the food was exactly the same in both, so I concluded that the difference must rest in the way it was cooked. Not that I had any choice in the matter: my total wealth amounted to one anvil, so I chose a suitable-looking canteen and went in. For somewhere to be properly suitable, of course, I would have preferred it to be completely empty. As a former officer-of-state in Greater Fallowfields I'd become accustomed to the luxury of dining alone. Here in the city, by contrast, it was necessary to share premises with other people. Moreover, they were all sitting in very close proximity to one another. The canteen I'd selected only had two or three empty tables, but I quickly recognised that I wasn't going to come across anywhere quieter at such a busy time of day. As it was, I almost lost my place before I started. Having seemingly reserved a table, I went and washed my hands only to return and find someone else had taken it. After that I made sure I was quicker off the mark: within a few minutes I had a table all to myself. What I couldn't help noticing, however, was that everyone behaved as though nobody else was in the room. For instance, there was a man sitting about two feet away on my right who reminded me slightly of Whimbrel. I was almost tempted to strike up a conversation with him, except that not once did he glance in my direction or even acknowledge my presence. He just sat silently minding his own business. The same applied to the man on my left, and the man to the left of him. In fact, no one paid the faintest attention to anybody else, so that each of us was effectively dining alone after all.

Before parting with my anvil I took a last look at the troublesome coin. It was odd to think that only a few weeks ago I had mistaken it for my stipendiary sixpence, which in its turn had made me feel like a man of importance. Now it was barely enough to buy my breakfast; and I realised that getting a job was no longer merely a convenient means for obtaining a travel permit: it was now a necessity. With these thoughts in mind I paid my bill and set off towards the employment exchange.

My hopes were immediately raised when I spotted Merganser going in the same direction. He was some distance ahead, so I hurried after him, knowing that this could be a good opportunity for me. If I could get to speak with him he'd most likely be able to fix something up and save the day. I was now gaining on him rapidly. He entered the building only a short while before I did, but when I got inside he'd vanished, presumably into some back room or other. Even so, the sighting gave me cause for renewed optimism: no doubt I would run into him again in the near future.

The employment exchange was arranged in a similar manner to the ticket hall. I had entered through a grand doorway, and now saw innumerable little windows with men sitting behind them. There were notices around the walls directing 'customers' to various sections, but I ignored these and approached the first window I came to. The man on the other side was wearing spectacles.

'Tell me you're a blacksmith,' he said. 'We're crying out for them at the moment.'

'Sorry,' I answered. 'No, I'm not.'

'A related trade, perhaps? Foundry man, drop forger, welder, riveter, turner?'

'No.'

'Are you any of these?' he said, reading from a list. 'Panel beater? Tinsmith? Coppersmith? Toolmaker?'

'No.'

'Boilermaker?'

'No.'

'Mechanic?'

'No.'

'Wheelwright? Cartwright? Cooper?'

'No.'

'What about construction? Stonemason? Bricklayer? Scaffolder? Joiner? Plasterer? Plumber? Painter? Decorator? Glazier? Roofer?'

'None of the above,' I said. 'Sorry.'

'No need to keep saying sorry,' he remarked. 'There's jobs a-plenty if we can just find you the right one. Now let's have a look.' He flipped briefly through a card index before resuming the interrogation. 'Baker? Confectioner? Pastry chef?'

'No.'

'Are you proficient in electrical circuitry?'

'No.'

'Telegraphy?'

'Never heard of it.'

'Dentistry?'

'No.'

'Weaving or spinning?'

'No.'

'The maintenance of clocks?'

'No.'

'Typesetting?'

'No.'

'Agriculture?'

'No.'

'Horticulture?'

'No.'

'Glassblowing?'

'No.'

The man paused and examined me over the rim of his spectacles.

'Are you a seamstress?' he asked.

'Certainly not,' I replied.

242

For a long moment he sat there with a furrowed brow. Then a thought occurred to him.

'Can you read and write?'

'Of course.'

'Well, I wish you'd said,' he said. 'We could have saved ourselves a lot of bother.' He referred to the very last card in his index. 'Here we are: a vacancy for a booking clerk.'

'Is that with the railway?' I enquired.

'No,' he said, 'it's with the municipal orchestra.'

22

I was given an address and a letter of introduction; also a map of the elevated tramline. This, apparently, circumnavigated the city at rooftop level. It could whisk passengers from one district to another in a matter of minutes. Unfortunately I had no money for the fare, so I had to walk. By way of consolation, I told myself that going on foot would help me get to know my new surroundings in more detail. Obviously I couldn't take in the whole place all at once, but a casual stroll on my first day would be a start. My destination was the civic concert hall; according to the map it was situated in Twenty-seventh Avenue. This in itself was a novelty. It seemed that the entire metropolis was laid out in an orderly grid with all the roads designated by a number or a letter from the alphabet. What a difference to Fallowfields, which was a maze of winding, higgledy-piggledy streets, some paved, some cobbled; and where any notion of planning was unheard of! I'd never thought about it before, but most of the street names in the imperial capital were completely baffling and gave no clue to one's whereabouts. Here in the City of Scoffers you knew that if you were standing in F-Street, then the neighbouring road would logically be called G-Street, and so on. In Fallowfields, by contrast, we had thoroughfares with names like Fire Engine Lane, Lost Sheep Crossing and Pudding Street Approach. I recalled that I once spent a fruitless afternoon searching in vain for Snakes and Ladders Yard. Subsequent investigation revealed that the so-called yard had long since been built over; it further transpired that Fire Engine Lane didn't have a fire station (neither, incidentally, did Pump Street or Helmet Row); Lost Sheep Crossing turned out to be a narrow passage where sheep couldn't possibly become lost; and Pudding Street Approach was nowhere near Pudding Street.

Now, as I stood looking along Alley No. 39, which was perfectly straight and ran parallel with Alley No. 38, I realised I was quite fond of chaotic, disorganised Fallowfields.

Nevertheless, I had to admit that the City of Scoffers was also impressive in its own way. Twenty-seventh Avenue was home to a number of enormous buildings. These included the Institute for Mathematical Excellence, the Hydrostatics Society and the headquarters of the CoS Railway Network.

The latter edifice caught my attention because of the huge banner hanging above the main entrance. It bore a forthright message in large black letters:

BUY RAILWAY BONDS

RESIST THE THREAT FROM THE WEST.

I couldn't imagine what sort of threat Fallowfields was supposed to be making to this formidable city. As far as I knew we were in no position to threaten anybody just now, what with our worthless currency reserves, our unpaid debt, our lack of ships and the prolonged absence of our emperor. Besides which, I'd have thought there was more to a successful society than simply expanding the railways. Surely they'd gone far enough already. What were they going to do when they reached the coast? Dig tunnels under the seabed? The idea was preposterous! I was coming to the conclusion that these 'scoffers' wasted a lot of energy on unnecessary projects, when they should be enjoying the finer things in life, as practised by people like Wryneck and Smew. Where, I wondered, were the museums, the libraries and the art galleries?

My question was answered when I reached the very next corner. Stretching for about half a mile between Twenty-seventh Avenue and J-Street was the City of Scoffers Museum of Fine Arts (incorporating the civic library).

'Well,' I reflected, 'I suppose at least that's something.'

After another ten minutes' walk I came to the concert hall. According to a sign at the top of the steps, this was the residence of the New Municipal Orchestra. It was also to be my workplace for the foreseeable future, so I headed up the steps and went inside. I had been informed at the employment exchange that I'd be answerable to the Professor of Music. There was an attendant on duty in the foyer. I introduced myself and he told me the professor was busy in his study. I would doubtless meet him in due course. Meanwhile he showed me into the box office and suggested I made myself familiar with the various types of ticket. The box office was small but comfortable. It had two windows: one overlooked the stone stairway outside; the other faced in towards the foyer. Directly opposite were the doors to the auditorium. Behind them I could hear the faint sound of an orchestra tuning their instruments; and for a poignant moment I was reminded of my former days of glory in Fallowfields. I also knew from experience that they were about to commence a rehearsal.

The ticketing arrangements looked simple enough to me, so after going through them a few times I emerged from the box office to stretch my legs. By now I'd managed to locate the Professor of Music's study. It was over in the far corner of the foyer, and I resolved to keep one eye on the door.

Positioned close to the box office was a noticeboard, its purpose presumably being to advertise upcoming events at the concert hall. For some reason it was completely bare at present, and I was just pondering this fact when the professor's door opened. Through it came Greylag.

His appearance had changed since our last encounter. Instead of his olive drab uniform he was now wearing a formal tail coat. As he came wandering into the foyer I experienced an odd sinking feeling. After all, Greylag was the individual on whom I now depended for my reference and travel permit. Quickly my mind ran back over the previous few months as I tried to remember exactly how I'd treated him. Had I been kind to him, unkind, or indifferent? If I had been unkind, would Greylag now be vengeful? I really couldn't tell. He had no knowledge of my failed attempts to purchase sweets for him and the other musicians. All he knew was that I'd allowed him to be transported to the City of Scoffers; and now the tables were well and truly turned.

I was relieved, therefore, when suddenly he recognised me and spoke in a friendly manner.

'Oh hello, sir,' he said. 'It's very nice to see you.'

'It's very nice to see you too,' I replied (I nearly added 'Professor Greylag', but I thought better of it).

In the same instant I realised that his mind was on far more important matters than vengeance. He had an orchestra to rehearse, and as always that was his priority. Furthermore, it occurred to me that Greylag's situation had changed much more drastically than mine. Only yesterday he'd been a serf in the Empire of Greater Fallowfields. Now he was Professor of Music in a rich and powerful city. No wonder, then, that he looked a little distracted.

'Are you all right?' I asked.

'Yes, thank you, sir,' he answered, 'but I'm afraid this professorship is taking some getting used to. I don't know anything about organising performances, selling tickets and so on. I'm just a musician, plain and simple.'

'Well, don't you worry about anything except the music,' I assured him. 'We'll take care of everything else.'

It gave me a nice feeling to be able to say this to Greylag, and he seemed slightly more at ease after our brief conversation. All the same I sensed that something else was troubling him. With regret I realised that I was hardly in a position to delve further. I was a humble booking clerk and he was my superior, so for the time being I would have to mind my own business.

Not long afterwards Greylag headed into the auditorium. Soon I heard the orchestra striking up, and I knew that for the moment at least he would be happy in his work.

For me, though, there was another revelation in store. Once Greylag had left me I resumed my duties in the box office. I'd been busy for about half an hour arranging the tickets according to their different colours when I happened to look out of the window. To my surprise I saw Sanderling at the top of the steps. He stood perfectly still, facing the street, with his hands clasped behind his back. He was wearing his dandy coat, and the buttons were fastened all the way up to the collar. I dashed straight outside to speak to him.

'Sanderling!' I said with glee.

'Greetings,' he replied.

'What are you doing here?'

'Front of house,' he said. 'They thought I looked the part.'

'Who did?'

'The people at the employment exchange.'

'Well, yes,' I said, glancing at his tightly buttoned coat, 'now you come to mention it you do.'

'Thanks.'

'How much are they paying you?'

'An anvil a day.'

'Same here,' I said.

Thus we were united in poverty.

However, it turned out we weren't as poor as we first imagined: our wages included free board and lodging. The accommodation was in an annexe at the rear of the concert hall, and a little later we went to have a look.

It was all rather disappointing. Priority had been given to members of the orchestra; Sanderling and I were a mere afterthought. Personally, I thought that the musicians were being unduly mollycoddled. They each had a private room with hot and cold running water and a view over the city. Sanderling and I, by contrast, had to share a kind of broom cupboard fitted with bunk beds. Also, we soon discovered that a tram went past our window every ten minutes. Despite these drawbacks, Sanderling was enthusiastic.

'We used to have bunk beds at the admiralty,' he said. 'They're great fun!'

Maybe so, but I suspected Sanderling was the sort of person who fidgeted about in bed. I had a feeling that if he lay in his bunk all night dreaming of dancing girls, it would be me who didn't get any sleep.

Over the next few days it became evident that there were influences bearing down on Greylag over which he had no control. He may have been Professor of Music but he did not have a completely free rein; quite the opposite in fact.

One morning there appeared on the noticeboard a programme of forthcoming performances. Apparently the orchestra would be playing the entire works of a composer who happened to be a former resident of the city. It was the centenary of his birth and the citizens wished to celebrate it with a music festival in his name.

Now this was all very well on the face of it: they were clearly proud of this man and regarded him as their greatest (perhaps only) composer. Nonetheless, as soon as I read the notice I began to have misgivings. This was the same composer whom Greylag had described to me as a 'fake' all those months ago. I remembered that he'd been totally dismissive of his first symphony and even suggested he'd made it up as he went along. Now Greylag was being asked to perform all of his works: the programme included nine symphonies, seven overtures, five quartets and three sonatas for piano and violin; also a tone poem and an orchestral concerto. Poor Greylag! He must have been in turmoil! Privately I conjectured that this was the real cause of his disquiet.

Even so, he gave the outward impression of someone who had embraced the festival wholeheartedly. First of all he researched and collated all the composer's manuscripts. He spent hours locked away in his study examining the relevant scores and preparing them for performance. Then he set about rehearsing the orchestra. It was going to take several weeks to work through the whole series, but by employing his usual thorough methods he was soon fully into his stride and the festival promised to be a success.

We received frequent visits from senior local figures, including Merganser, Gadwall and Grosbeak. They constantly enquired about the progress that Greylag was making; they asked if he was happy with conditions in the concert hall; and they reminded him that if there was anything he required he only needed to ask. By thus encouraging Greylag I speculated whether they were seeking reflected glory, in the way I had unashamedly in the recent past, or if they indeed believed in the talents of their home-grown composer. He was, after all, fairly famous; we even knew his name in Greater Fallowfields.

Personally, I quite liked some of the tunes I heard in rehearsals, but I'd learned during my tenure at the cake that tunes alone were not enough. Greylag's search for melodic discipline had taken him far beyond mere 'tunes'. His compositions allowed much more generous living space for his melodies, and this was the difference between his work and the collection currently on offer. I noticed at the beginning of each rehearsal that Greylag drew a deep breath as if bracing himself against what was to come. It was plain to me that he underwent a kind of torture whenever he performed these pieces, but his patrons never guessed a thing. Occasionally they looked in at practice sessions, standing inconspicuously (or so they thought) in the shadows. Afterwards, when they departed, they never failed to give nods of approval.

Meanwhile, posters started to appear all over the surrounding area: the composer's portrait was to become increasingly familiar over the ensuing weeks. Even Sanderling was aware that there was a big festival drawing near, though as usual he managed to get hold of the wrong end of the stick.

'I presume there'll be dancing as well as music, will there?' he ventured late one evening as we lay in our respective bunks.

'Possibly,' I said. 'It depends who turns up.'

'Yes,' he said, 'I suppose you're right.'

He didn't pursue the subject further, but for the remainder of the night he was particularly restless.

Judging by ticket sales the event was guaranteed to be a triumph. No sooner had I opened the box office on the first day of booking than long queues began to form. Sanderling had his work cut out keeping everyone in line. He was also required to clear the way for visiting dignitaries who came demanding seats in the grand tier. I wondered if any of them had the habit of coughing during quiet passages; or maybe such lapses had been abolished in the City of Scoffers.

That wouldn't have surprised me at all. The entire place ticked along like clockwork, and anything which jeopardised its smooth operation was dealt with immediately. Rules and regulations were applied to the letter; correct procedures were invariably followed; and, of course, the trains always ran on time. As a matter of fact, from what I could gather it was the railways which were the governing force here. Virtually every aspect of daily life was imbued with their influence: the dictatorship of the clocks was endemic and unavoidable. Standard Railway Time applied throughout the year; the length of a day had nothing to do with natural occurrences such as sunrise and sunset. Instead, the hours were numbered simply from one to twenty-four, the terms 'noon' and 'midnight' having long since been abandoned. Great towering floodlights illuminated the industrial areas, and industry in general made no attempt to be quiet during hours of darkness. All the factories and mills had their own shunting yards; accordingly, workers' shift patterns revolved around the arrivals and departures of freight. The elevated tramline functioned in harmony with the railways; so did the postal system and the network for the delivery of milk. Everybody carried a pocket watch or similar timepiece (this was compulsory), but actually you could tell the time from the hoots and whistles of passing engines. Even the forthcoming concerts were scheduled to coincide with train services (not the other way round). Such was the scoffers' obsession with time that every rehearsal was attended by a uniformed man holding a stopwatch. He recorded the exact duration of each symphony, overture or sonata; the results were then posted outside the concert hall each evening, presumably so that the audience knew in advance when the music would end. Greylag seemed quite bemused when he first noticed the man with the stopwatch, but after a while he just ignored him.

Even so, the importance of the railways couldn't be denied. We had already seen its effect in the empire: our clocks had been changed, our currency undermined and our population depleted; and yet Fallowfields only occupied one branch of a vast structure. The City of Scoffers had a reach which extended in many other directions too. How many realms, I pondered, now lay under its 'protection'? Was there any limit to its policy of continual enlargement? Obviously not. The railways developed alongside the industries they were built to serve. Each created demands on the other, and the only solution was perpetual expansion.

The consequences could be seen every day at the central railway station. Hordes of migrants disembarked from countless trains, all clutching their 'recruiting sixpences'. I soon got into the routine of wandering down to the station every morning to see if I recognised any of the new arrivals. I wasn't sure who I expected to see: definitely not Whimbrel, but I wouldn't have been surprised if Dotterel or Garganey had shown up, attracted merely by curiosity. In the event neither of them did, but there were plenty of other Fallowfieldsmen to make up the number. They were easily distinguishable because even though they all wore identical olive drab uniforms, they all looked completely different to one another. The purpose of a uniform, as I understood it, was to make everybody seem alike, but for some reason this precept didn't apply to my compatriots. Some of them looked downright scruffy despite their uniforms being crisply pressed and brand new from the factory; others wore their uniforms in their own personal style; for example, with the cuffs rolled back or the collar turned up. Still others had been given outfits which were plainly the wrong size for them. One individual set his look off with a jaunty cap; another displayed a sprig of heather in his buttonhole. They were all typical Fallowfieldsmen, yet their collective appearance was hardly consistent with the notion of uniformity.

What these men had in common, of course, was their new destination. They all came in hope: some naturally to be disappointed; others to succeed. How many had been recruited unfairly I didn't know, but in any case it was too late now.

There was no going back without a train ticket, and you couldn't get one of those without a travel permit.

If you wanted a job, on the other hand, this was unquestionably the place to come. The City of Scoffers was confident and unabashed. Above its proud buildings fluttered the hammer and anvil, symbol of its industrial might. The people went about with pocketfuls of money which they spent freely, thus generating even more wealth. The process was seemingly unstoppable.

Nevertheless, I sensed there was a chink in the armour. It was hardly anything, but it was there all right: a hidden uncertainty lurking behind the apparent success. Whimbrel had first drawn my attention to it weeks earlier when he mentioned the stream of visitors to the observatory. They all wished to peer through his telescope, and without exception they turned it to the west, never explaining why. Similarly, here in the city was the banner urging people to buy railway bonds and 'resist the threat from the west'. It hung outside the headquarters of the CoS Railway Network, somewhere I'd have thought of as a veritable stronghold. Yet to my ears the appeal sounded almost fearful.

I glanced at this banner whenever I passed by, not least because I was astounded by the sheer size of it. Then, one bright and breezy morning, I noticed the wording had been changed. Now it simply said:

THERE IS NO ALTERNATIVE TO TRAINS.

I looked at the banner a second time, just to make sure I hadn't read it wrongly; then I continued on my way, trying to work out just what lay behind this strident claim. Needless to say, there *was* an alternative to trains – namely, shipping – but as we were so far from the sea I allowed them this error. Moreover, if it was purely a matter of railways versus canals, then obviously the statement was correct: canals became obsolete as a means of transport the moment the first length of track was laid.

I got the impression, however, that an element of self-doubt had emerged about investing solely in railways: were they trying to convince themselves they hadn't taken the wrong course? Well, if they had they should have thought about it years ago. As far as the City of Scoffers was concerned there was indeed no alternative to trains, but they didn't need to shout it from the rooftops.

Still, there was little time to contemplate the subject further. The day of the first concert had arrived, so I hurried back to take up my post in the box office (I didn't really expect any 'returns' but you never could tell). It had been decided that the festival would open with a matinée *and* an evening performance. Greylag was scheduled to present a symphony at three in the afternoon, followed by another at eight o'clock. It was a heavy workload, but he seemed not the slightest bit overawed.

Sanderling, by contrast, was very much on edge.

'All those people streaming in,' he said. 'How can I possibly check their tickets and show them to their seats?'

'Don't worry about it,' I advised. 'Most people sort their seats out themselves.'

Fortunately for Sanderling, I was proved right. The matinée audience arrived punctually and remained in good order as they filed into the auditorium. I half-expected the occasion to be marked by a speech, delivered perhaps by Grosbeak or Merganser. They were both present, as was Gadwall, but apparently they weren't interested in any flummery. The orchestra was already in position, and at precisely three o'clock the concert started without any announcements. Just as the lights dimmed I slid in at the back to watch Greylag in action. As usual he displayed perfect control over the orchestra. Interestingly enough, this first symphony matched exactly the verbal description he'd given me all those months before. It was a little unsettling to watch him perform it so flawlessly, knowing that all the while he held it in such disdain. When the music finally ended he gave a bow, the audience applauded and the concert hall emptied.

The second performance went equally smoothly, but afterwards Sanderling was completely exhausted and had to be revived with a bottle of wine. We'd discovered during our short time in the city that you could buy anything if you had the money, so we'd decided initially on this shared bottle.

'I really ought to save up,' he said. 'I don't intend to drink all my wages away.'

'No,' I said, 'nor me.'

We agreed mutually that fairly soon we should consider rationing ourselves. In the meantime we would try to be as useful as possible, thereby ensuring our continued employment.

Following the introductory back-to-back concerts, the festival reverted to a more leisurely programme of two performances a week. Obviously, the orchestra needed to rehearse each piece thoroughly, but there was also time for Greylag to resume work on his own compositions. Occasionally I would enter the auditorium and recognise snatches I hadn't heard since we were at the cake. It was gratifying to know that Greylag was still pushing at the boundaries, as befitted an appointed Professor of Music.

So it was that our existence gradually evolved into a regular cycle. The orchestra rehearsed, practised and performed; the audiences came and went; Sanderling and I sold tickets and took care of the concert hall as it filled and emptied again. At the end of each day we drank a bottle of wine and then went to bed.

I soon noticed that Sanderling was starting to take an active interest in the performances themselves. Often I saw him chatting to Greylag during recesses, and it turned out he was enquiring about the differing musical forms that were being showcased during the festival. After a while he commenced taking notes, firstly for his own clarification, but later for the enlightenment of others. On subsequent concert evenings he could be observed imparting his newly acquired knowledge to chosen members of the audience. Clearly he was enjoying his role as 'front of house'. Each afternoon between two and four he slipped away, having presumably found somewhere quiet to revise his notes.

Eventually, with the final symphony approaching, I began to wonder what we were supposed to do when the festival was over. Hopefully there were many future programmes in prospect, but the City of Scoffers was now in the depths of winter and I had a feeling they wouldn't come to fruition until the spring. The skies darkened and the days were cold. New arrivals at the central station appeared half-perished, yet still they kept pouring in. The city's flags fluttered and became ragged in the bitter easterly wind.

For the time being, though, life remained satisfactory. After all, the concert hall was comparatively cosy. Soft pink chandeliers glowed all day long while the orchestra rehearsed, and Greylag was as fully absorbed as ever. The ninth symphony was the longest of the works he was performing; hence he spent many hours labouring over its four movements. Then, at last, he was ready.

Tickets for the closing concert had been sold out days earlier. On the evening of the performance there were crowds gathering at the door long before dusk. Sanderling was there keeping order and telling people what they already knew: that this was their cherished composer's most well-known symphony. Finished only days before he died, it was generally considered his departing masterpiece. The anticipation of the audience was palpable. By eight o'clock we had them all sitting comfortably inside. The orchestra was waiting; the lights were dimmed and Greylag made his entrance. At the last moment a latecomer sidled into the only empty seat. Sanderling and I took up our positions standing at the rear of the house.

I sometimes thought Greylag was rather cruel in his assessment of this composer. While I was quite aware of his own exacting standards, it seemed to me that he gave insufficient quarter to rival composers, especially this one. As I stood listening to the ninth symphony I heard only pleasant tunes, dynamic phrases and an overarching theme that was hardly forgettable. Sadly, I concluded that Greylag's years in serfdom must have shaped his opinion of others.

By now the symphony was moving towards its finale. I knew from rehearsals that it didn't end with a climactic eruption as with most similar works. Instead the fourth movement petered out quietly, leaving the listener to reflect on what had gone before. When the last notes faded away the audience sat in silence for a few seconds; then they responded with thunderous applause. Greylag turned towards them, bowed, and left the podium.

Hitherto during the festival there had been no encores. Apparently they weren't customary in the City of Scoffers. I had witnessed the occasional standing ovation, usually after the more famous pieces, but that was more or less the extent of their enthusiasm. These were serious people: they were not given to prolonged bouts of floor-stamping.

Tonight, however, was different. Maybe it was because the music had been so powerful, or simply that this was the final performance of the festival: whatever the reason, the audience demanded an encore. The applause continued unabated until Greylag reappeared at last. He even received a muted cheer from one or two people down at the front. Then everyone fell silent.

Evidently he'd chosen the purest course of action: he proceeded to play the fourth movement once again. This was most agreeable. We'd only heard it a few minutes before, yet in Greylag's hands it sounded as fresh as if it had just been written. Towards the end, though, some sort of change had been made: not to the music itself, but to the instrumentation. The main theme from the first movement had returned and the whole orchestra was in full flight when suddenly all the cellos stopped playing. As the other musicians continued, the cellists packed away their instruments and left the arena. After a few more bars, the entire brass section did exactly the same thing; but Greylag went on conducting as if nothing had happened. I glanced at Sanderling and he raised his eyebrows; then we carried on watching in fascination. Slowly but surely, different parts of the orchestra began to disappear, each musician carefully putting his instrument in its case prior to departing. The oboes went next, then some of the percussion, then the rest of the woodwind. The dwindling orchestra played on as the symphony's conclusion drew gradually closer. Soon there were only a half dozen violins remaining; then three; then only two. In the original piece the entire ensemble had delivered the last few bars very quietly. This time we were carried to the end by a lone violin. He finished playing and packed away his instrument. Then he, too, vanished. Finally, Greylag turned to the audience, gave a bow and left his podium.

Fortunately, the onlookers took it all in good humour. After an initial stunned silence they began clapping again, louder and louder, until genuine applause had fully returned.

Clearly they viewed it as an interesting diversion with no added connotations.

Yet from where I stood the message was obvious. I leant over to Sanderling and spoke in his ear: 'Greylag wants to go home.'

23

Once the crowds had departed, I went into the auditorium to sweep up the discarded tickets. I expected the place to be empty: most people had trains to catch and stragglers were unheard of in the City of Scoffers. I was doubly surprised, therefore, to see Wryneck sitting in one of the seats. He was lounging at the back of the stalls, and appeared to be scrutinising the arched ceiling.

When he caught my gaze he nodded.

'The acoustics here are far superior to those in the cake,' he remarked.

'Yes,' I said, 'I don't doubt it.'

He rose from his seat and began strolling around the auditorium. He peered at the pink chandeliers and classical decor. Then he went up to the grand tier and examined the quality of the upholstery. Finally, he mounted the conductor's podium. He stood for a moment conducting an imaginary orchestra before joining me in the stalls.

'This is the standard we'll be seeking when the cake is restored,' he announced.

Wryneck spoke as if we were continuing a conversation we'd broken off only a few minutes earlier, rather than renewing an acquaintanceship after several long weeks, but this was typical of him. He rarely bothered with such trifles as saying hello.

'Enjoy the concert, did you?' I asked.

'Excellent,' he replied.

'How did you manage to get a ticket?'

'On the black market.'

'I didn't know there was one.'

'Oh yes,' he said, 'you can buy anything here if you have the money.'

Despite Wryneck's supercilious manner I was quite pleased to see him again. He was wearing his dandy coat, and the sight of it brought back memories of life in Fallowfields. I thought fondly of Whimbrel pottering around in the observatory; of Gallinule and his companions drinking in the Maypole; and of glorious sunlit evenings in the great library.

'How's Smew?' I enquired. 'Does he still have lemon curd for tea?'

'He's fine,' replied Wryneck, 'but the lemon curd ran out.'

'Oh dear.'

'So did the quince marmalade and the fortified wine.'

'So you're here for the black market, are you?'

'No,' said Wryneck, 'I've come to find that young emperor of ours.'

The emperor! I'd forgotten all about him. His alleged antics at the university had led indirectly to all the recent upheavals: the occupation of the imperial capital; the resulting shortages; the displacement of the orchestra; not to mention my own sojourn here in the City of Scoffers. Yet for some reason he'd completely slipped my mind. It was odd to think that he was playing truant somewhere in the metropolis while the rest of us got on with our lives as best we could. Now, all of a sudden, Wryneck had turned up on a mission to find him and bring him to book. Or at least that was the presumed intention. His tone of voice certainly suggested he'd lost patience with our elusive sovereign. It transpired, however, that Wryneck wasn't here simply to mete out chastisement. Seemingly, the person of the emperor was required for critical reasons of state.

'We have reached a low ebb,' Wryneck explained, 'but there is a chance the situation can be saved. A few weeks back we received word that a great fleet of ships had landed on the western seashore. An envoy was dispatched and he returned with some remarkable news. The landing party claimed they were descended from the mariners who sailed into the west all those years ago. Evidently their forebears discovered a plentiful new world and soon became prosperous, but now some of them wish to return to the empire.'

Wryneck paused and smiled to himself before continuing.

'These people aren't a bit like us but they insist that they're our closest cousins. I've met them and they appear to be very earnest, though I must say they take some getting used to. They speak in superlatives, they walk with a swagger and they constantly refer to themselves as "liberators". Their wealth is derived from a range of processes we've never even thought of, and for some reason they want to share it with us. They took one look at the railway and instantly offered to buy it; they propose to restore the cake to its former glory; and they want to establish an automotive industry in Fallowfields.'

'That's all good news then,' I remarked.

'Good news indeed,' said Wryneck, 'except that they added a precondition.'

'Which is?'

'Greater Fallowfields must have a reputable cabinet headed by the emperor himself.'

'So that's why you're here.'

'Correct.'

'How on earth are you going to find him?'

'Good question,' said Wryneck. 'Obviously we can't hope for any assistance from the local authorities: if we succeed they'll have to give the orchestra back.'

'Yes, I suppose they will.'

Wryneck glanced around the auditorium.

'Actually, that's why I came here tonight,' he said. 'I thought there was a possibility the emperor might wish to see his orchestra perform the famous ninth. The event has been advertised all over the city so he was bound to have known about it.'

'Yes, he must have.'

'Apparently, however, my high expectations were ill-founded: I saw nobody of his description.'

'Well,' I said, 'someone did sneak in just after the lights were dimmed. Maybe that was him.'

'No,' said Wryneck, 'it was me.'

'Ah.'

'I'd been following a line of inquiry and it made me late.'

'Did anybody check your ticket?'

'No.'

'Then I'd better have a look,' I said. 'I ought to know what these forgeries are like.'

'Oh, I don't think it's a forgery,' said Wryneck.

'It must be,' I retorted. 'I was in charge of the box office and I wouldn't have sold tickets to anyone who looked unscrupulous.'

'See for yourself.'

Wryneck handed me his ticket and I examined it closely. True enough, it exactly resembled the tickets I'd been issuing all these weeks; which suggested that somebody had sold it under the counter.

'But there's only been me and Sanderling here,' I said, 'and he would never stoop to such depths.'

Wryneck regarded me for a long moment.

'That reminds me,' he said, 'I need to speak to Sanderling about the arrangements for tomorrow.'

'Oh yes?'

'As a matter of fact I'm quite indebted to him: he's really been most obliging during my search for the emperor. He helped me contact some dancing girls with whom he was intimate.'

'Sanderling?'

'No, the emperor.'

'Good grief.'

'I've been conducting interviews every afternoon between two and four.'

'Any luck?'

'Not yet,' said Wryneck, 'but I intend to persevere.'

These revelations all came as a bit of a shock to me. Plainly Sanderling was a much darker horse than I'd imagined. Moreover, Wryneck was proving himself to be a very astute customer. Whether he'd taken matters into his own hands or was acting under Smew's orders I wasn't sure. Either way, it appeared likely that I'd soon be going back to Fallowfields to resume my seat in the cabinet; which meant I'd have to apply to Greylag for a travel permit. Technically he was still my employer, and I realised I needed to play this game very carefully over the next few days. Without any further explanation, Wryneck wandered off in search of Sanderling, leaving me to ponder his words.

So, Greater Fallowfields was to be liberated, was it? Well, perhaps; but I wondered at what price a final settlement would be achieved. These newcomers had begun making demands already, and I suspected that the empire was in danger of becoming a mere puppet state.

For the moment, of course, the whole subject remained in abeyance. Our priority was to find the emperor as soon as possible. The following day Wryneck renewed his investigations; I offered to accompany him but he politely informed me that Sanderling's contacts were more valuable. The two of them departed shortly after breakfast.

Finding myself at a loose end, I dropped in on the musicians to see how they were getting on. To my astonishment the auditorium was deserted. In all the time I'd been attached to the orchestra I had never known them not to practise or rehearse, but today they were all absent. A short investigation revealed that some of them were still in bed, while others had gone sightseeing. Well, I had to admit they deserved it: they'd done nothing but work, work, work ever since I'd known them and clearly they needed a rest. What surprised me, though, was that they didn't bother unpacking their instruments for the entire day. When they returned in the evening a good few of them had red faces and smelt of drink; it then dawned on me that they must have been out spending their wages. Obviously this would have been an experience for which they were poorly prepared, and doubtless they'd regret it in the morning.

I was then struck by a secondary thought: if the musicians were indeed going home, as now seemed probable, how would the new regime react to having an orchestra of serfs on its hands? Serfdom hardly fitted in with the idea of liberation as I understood it, and suddenly I pictured a lot of unanswered questions. Where, for example, would Greylag stand in all this?

It so happened he was difficult to track down too. Naturally, I expected him to exclude himself from any sort of holidaymaking, and guessed he would resort to the privacy of his study. Yet when I knocked on the door there was no reply. I noticed the door was off its catch, so gently I pushed it open and peered inside. The room was empty.

After some thought I remembered that Greylag had been greatly inspired by the railway engine we'd seen on our jaunt into the countryside; he'd composed some highly experimental music on the strength of it. Accordingly, I thought I might seek him out at the central station. When I got there the usual flurry of activity appeared to have abated slightly: although the coming and going never ceased, it was nowhere near the level I was accustomed to. A glance at the timetable told me a train was due to arrive from Fallowfields in the next few minutes, so I went to the designated platform. Sure enough, standing at the far end was a lone figure. When I drew nearer, however, I realised that it wasn't Greylag, but Grosbeak. He stood immobile, except for an occasional glance at his pocket watch, and gazed steadfastly towards the west. I assumed he was waiting for a specific passenger or group of passengers; therefore, I stayed where I was and watched with interest. After another minute a whistle sounded in the distance. Then the rails began to hum as the train approached. Grosbeak continued to stand stock still, apparently lost in thought. I could now see the engine clearly: it had obviously received a new coat of paint recently and was gleaming in the pale winter sunshine. I also observed that it had been given a name: emblazoned along the side in bright gold lettering were the words EMPIRE OF FALLOWFIELDS.

The train pulled importantly into the platform, but when it came to a halt I saw that it was completely empty.

Dusk had descended when I returned to the concert hall. The lights in the foyer were glowing dimly, and from inside the auditorium I heard music being played. I looked in and saw Greylag sitting at the piano as if he'd been there all day. He was composing a nocturne by the sound of it, and every so often he would pause and make some changes to his man-uscript. It was heartening to know that some things would never change in Greylag's world. I decided this should be cel-ebrated, so I went to the broom cupboard and collected a bottle of wine and two glasses. (The wine actually belonged half to Sanderling and half to me, but under the circumstances I felt he was hardly in a position to complain if I opened it.) I returned to the auditorium and poured a glass for Greylag and one for myself.

To my surprise Greylag refused his glass.

'Not when I'm playing, thank you all the same,' he said. 'It seems somewhat unprofessional.'

So I sat under the pink chandeliers and drank alone, listen-ing while Greylag resumed work on his nocturne. He was just about finished when Wryneck and Sanderling came back. It was very late and Sanderling looked quite flushed. The pair of them were disconsolate.

'No luck then?' I ventured.

'I'm afraid not,' replied Wryneck. 'The trail appears to have gone cold.'

'We've tried everywhere,' added Sanderling, 'but nobody's seen the emperor; not lately anyway.'

'So what are we going to do?' I asked.

'There's only one solution,' said Wryneck. 'We'll have to find a substitute.'

24

The cake looked truly magnificent in the early spring sunshine. The restoration work had been completed to a high standard and the results were impressive.

Not a moment too soon, by all accounts.

No one in the empire ever noticed that the stone walls had begun gradually to fade over the years. It had required the eyes of outsiders, of course, to recognise the problem and rectify it. Now that they'd been returned to their original yellow hue we could plainly see the difference. Another decade, apparently, and they would have started to crumble.

Meanwhile, the roof had been cleared of all the dead leaves and other detritus which marred its creamy-white dome.

Now, once again, the cake appeared good enough to eat!

Performances would resume when all the seats had been reinstalled. (Nobody liked the idea of having to stand to watch the orchestra play.)

25

As the clock struck ten, Shrike opened the register.

'Let us begin,' he said. 'Chancellor of the Exchequer?'

'Present,' said Sanderling.

'Postmaster General?'

'Present,' said Whimbrel.

'Astronomer Royal?'

'Present,' I said.

'Comptroller for the Admiralty?'

'Present,' said Smew.

'Surveyor of the Imperial Works?'

'Present,' said Mestolone.

'Pellitory-of-the-Wall?'

'Present,' said Wryneck.

'Principal Composer to the Imperial Court?'

'Present,' said Greylag.

'His Exalted Highness, the Majestic Emperor of the Realms, Dominions, Colonies and Commonwealth of Greater Fallowfields?'

Shrike paused and waited.

Five minutes went slowly by and nothing happened. Then suddenly there was a huge fuss and kerfuffle outside the door.

'Let us pass!' demanded an imperious voice. 'We are the Player King!'

The author would like to thank Simon Moody
and Mark Pappenheim for their patience.

A NOTE ON THE AUTHOR

Magnus Mills is the author of *The Restraint of Beasts*, which won the McKitterick Prize and was shortlisted for both the Booker Prize and the Whitbread First Novel Award in 1998, and of five other novels, including *The Scheme for Full Employment*, and the story collection *Screwtop Thompson*. He lives in London.

A NOTE ON THE TYPE

The text of this book is set in Bembo. This type was first used in 1495 by the Venetian printer Aldus Manutius for Cardinal Bembo's *De Aetna*, and was cut for Manutius by Francesco Griffo. It was one of the types used by Claude Garamond (1480–1561) as a model for his Romain de L'Université, and so it was the fore-runner of what became standard European type for the following two centuries. Its modern form follows the original types and was designed for Monotype in 1929.